MOON
ASTROLOGY

This book is dedicated to the memory of Kieran Hudson, who passed to the Great Mystery at full moon on 22 May 2005, when this book was first in production, and to his mother, Cally, whose sun and moon are both in moon-ruled Cancer. Good journey, Kieran. Blessings of the Goddess, Cally.

An Hachette UK Company
www.hachette.co.uk

First published in Great Britain in
2006 by Godsfield Press, an imprint of
Octopus Publishing Group Ltd
Carmelite House, 50 Victoria
Embankment, London EC4Y 0DZ
www.octopusbooks.co.uk

This edition published in 2023

Copyright © Octopus Publishing Group
Ltd 2006, 2020, 2023
Text copyright © Teresa Dellbridge 2006,
2020, 2023

Distributed in the US by
Hachette Book Group
1290 Avenue of the Americas
4th and 5th Floors
New York, NY 10104

Distributed in Canada by
Canadian Manda Group
664 Annette St.
Toronto, Ontario, Canada M6S 2C8

ISBN 978-1-8418-1532-9

A CIP catalogue record for this book is
available from the British Library

Printed and bound in China

10 9 8 7 6 5 4 3 2 1

Publisher: Lucy Pessell
Designer: Isobel Platt
Editor: Hannah Coughlin
Assistant Editor: Samina Rahman
Production Controllers:
Lucy Carter and Nic Jones

MOON ASTROLOGY

using the moon's signs and phases to enhance your life

TERESA DELLBRIDGE

GODSFIELD

CONTENTS

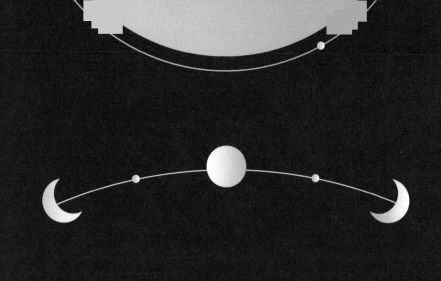

INTRODUCTION

The moon is our closest neighbour in space. In fact the earth and moon are, in a sense, 'sisters' because they form a system together. We tend to assume that the moon goes around the earth, but the gravitational pull of the moon is such that the earth also moves in tune with it, in a cosmic dance.

The moon has given rise to many myths and stories throughout the ages. It is a friend to trysting lovers, a muse to poets and artists, and in the eerie light of full moon it is easy to believe that spirits roam the skies. Most important of all, astrologers believe that the moon influences life on earth in many ways: from creating the twice-daily tides of our oceans to affecting our very personalities and moods. Becoming aware of this can help you to live and enjoy your life to the fullest.

Moon astrology connects you to your instincts and intuitions. It helps you to attune to the subtle rhythms of life and to use these to good effect. Learning about what is called your moon sign (see page 8) will put you in touch with hidden aspects of yourself, and finding out about lunar phases and their meanings will enable you to draw on ancient wisdom and be more effectual, serene and wise on your journey through life.

WHAT IS MOON ASTROLOGY?

Astrology is the art of interpreting the movements of heavenly bodies in relation to their links with life on earth. Most people are aware of at least one aspect of astrology – that which concerns the sun.

The sun takes a whole year to move around what is known as the zodiac. 'Zodiac', meaning 'circle of animals', is the band of sky within which the sun, the moon and all the planets are seen to move. It is divided into twelve well-known areas, called the signs of the zodiac, each named after the constellation of stars that once lay in it (see page 20). The signs and constellations no longer coincide because of a complex astronomical phenomenon called the Precession of the Equinoxes. However, the signs still apply as they are based on cosmic rhythms rather than literal pictures in the sky. The sun takes about a month to move through one of the signs, and the sign that the sun is in at the time of your birth becomes your familiar 'sun sign' or 'star sign'. You probably know about the characteristics of your sun sign and can relate many of them to

your personality. However, true astrology takes account of the positions of all the planets, and, most especially, the moon.

MOON SIGNS

The first aspect of moon astrology concerns what is called the 'moon sign' at the time of your birth. When you were born, the moon – as well as the sun – was in one of the signs of the zodiac. In contrast to the sun, however, the moon takes only two-and-a-half days to move through an entire sign, as opposed to a month. This means that your moon sign is more specific: someone born only a couple of days after you will have a different moon sign. This is one of many reasons why people born under the same 'sun' or 'star' sign can have very different characteristics. The moon, when you were born, may have been in a sign very much in contrast to your sun sign. It all helps to make you the interesting, complex person that you are.

CONSTANT MOVEMENT

The second aspect of moon astrology is the perpetual movement of the moon from sign to sign. The fact that it moves around the zodiac all the time, taking just two-and-a-half days to move through each of the twelve signs and almost a month to go the whole way around the zodiac, means that the influence of the moon on the earth alters every two-and-a-half days, bringing different energies and constantly affecting how we feel (see page 10).

LUNAR PHASES

The third application of moon astrology deals with the phases of the moon. These are caused by the changing position of the moon in the sky, relative to the sun and earth, and have no direct relationship to the zodiac. No matter what phase the moon is in, the half nearest the sun is always lit up. However, we cannot always see this half due to the earth's position, so only certain portions of it are visible to us at different times. Over the course of every 29-and-a-half days the moon, as we see it, passes from dark and new moon, through waxing (first quarter) to full moon,

and through waning (third quarter) back to dark and new moon again.

The different phases of the moon over the course of a month will become quite obvious once you are tuned into them – a dark moon cannot be seen at all, a new moon appears as a thin silver crescent in the evening, a fuller waxing moon is visible later in the evening, a full moon is directly overhead at around midnight, and a wan, shrinking moon isn't visible until the small hours of the morning. What may not be so readily observed is the fact that these phases affect the rhythms of life on the earth, to which people, animals, plants, the oceans and the planet itself respond. It is important to reconnect not only with the meanings of your individual moon sign, but also with the energy fluctuations of the lunar phases and the effect that they have on your life, planning what you do accordingly, as many people are believed to have done in ancient times.

HOW MOON ASTROLOGY WORKS

Using the simple charts on pages 132–141 to discover your own moon sign will give you insight into a whole new aspect of yourself. Although your lunar nature is part of your life – and indeed may be more obvious to your nearest and dearest than your sun sign – the chances are you have overlooked it because it relates to your instincts and habits, and you probably just express these automatically, never really analysing what you are doing and feeling.

Your moon sign relates to a very basic part of your nature, which reacts according to needs and feelings, gets into moods and grooves, has intuitions, and irrational impulses and perceptions. It is also linked to the way you love, nurture and play. You may consciously develop your sun sign nature, but your lunar nature tends to peep out in moments when you are relaxed and is often most obvious when you are at home, unwinding. Your lunar nature may also take over in times of stress. It needs to be satisfied for you to be effectual; otherwise, inner frustrations may trip you up. When you have discovered your moon sign in the charts, you can begin to get acquainted with your lunar needs, know and understand

yourself better and become a more complete individual.

The moon's position when you were born imprinted your instinctual nature, but its ever-changing position also affects your life on a day-to-day basis: its monthly journey through the signs of the zodiac brings constant shifts of mood and atmosphere to which we are all sensitive. When the moon is passing through the same sign that it was in at the time of your birth, for example, you could feel more emotional; when it is in a harmonious sign, you are likely to be in a good mood; and when it is in a challenging sign, you might feel irritable or uneasy. For instance, if you were born with the moon in restless Sagittarius, you may feel that you are blocked at every turn when the moon is passing through stolid Taurus, but energized by a fiery Aries moon.

If we were to view our lives as a painting, the moon sign gives the background colouring, while the moon's phases are the individual brushstrokes. Or, to use a musical metaphor, the sign is the underlying melody, while the phases are the fluctuating volume and beat, pulsating like a heartbeat throughout the earth.

Each phase of the moon brings its own gifts, strengths and uses; each is necessary in the grand scheme of things, and – since they depend on the relationship between the sun, moon and earth, not the place from which you are viewing the sky – the phases are the same all over the earth. When it is full moon in London: it is full moon in Tokyo, Sydney and New York, too: the entire earth responds to the moon in unison.

LUNAR PHASES

DARK MOON –NEW MOON

A 'dark moon' – which is invisible to us – occurs when the earth, moon and sun are almost in a straight line, with the moon in the middle. We cannot see the moon because the half of it lit up by the sun is facing away from the earth – towards the sun. When the line-up is truly straight (about every six months), a solar eclipse occurs, wherein the moon casts its shadow onto the earth's surface. Depending on how exact the line-up is, and how far the moon is from the earth (for this varies a little), the eclipse will be either total or partial. However, a solar eclipse can only be seen over an area of up to about 270 km (170 miles), as this is the maximum width of the moon's shadow where it touches the earth, which means eclipses are few and far between in any one place.

Eclipses used to be viewed as a bad omen as people thought the lights of the heavens were being swallowed up. For example, famine, disease and the imminent death of the king were just a few interpretations. Perhaps the fact that a solar eclipse can only take place during a dark moon is one of the reasons that this phase is still considered inauspicious by some people. Generally, dark moon is a time of inwardness, quiet, deep thought and reduced activity (see pages 48–49). The terms 'dark moon' and 'new moon' are combined for the purposes of this book, for as soon as the moon moves past the sun, it starts on a 'new' journey, reflecting the light of the sun on its edge. At this stage the new moon is seen as that hopeful silver bow in the evening sky.

WAXING MOON

Now the phase of waxing moon commences, during which the first quarter moon occurs. This is when more and more of the moon becomes visible, and is a time of growth and increased energy in our lives. The moon rises later and later each evening and becomes more and more round, until, eventually, the edge of the moon that is furthest from the sun is completely revealed, revealing a full moon. It is important to note that the moon is seen to wax from right to left in the northern hemisphere, so that a crescent moon could be cupped by a curved right palm, fingers pointing upwards; whereas the moon is seen to wax from left to right in the southern hemisphere, so that a crescent moon could be cupped in the left palm.

FULL MOON

A full moon is bright white and circular, and appears in the centre of the sky at midnight. This is a magical time, full of fruition, when the earth and moon are again in a straight line, but this time with the earth in the middle. When the line-up is exact, a lunar eclipse will take place, wherein the moon turns deep-red due to being in the shadow of the earth. Since the earth is larger than the moon, lunar eclipses can take up to two hours and are visible all over the part of the earth where it is night, while solar eclipses are only visible over a limited area. Lunar eclipses were a cause of great fear in the past, as the blood-coloured moon seemed a harbinger of destruction. It looked like the lights in the heavens were being 'eaten up', and even today lunar eclipses can create a disturbing feeling. However, because the moon did not seem as vital to life as the sun, its disappearance was not quite so alarming.

WANING MOON

After the full moon comes the waning of the moon. As the portion of the moon that we can see decreases, so too do our energies tend to ebb or turn within. The moon moves into its third quarter, shrinks and pales, rising later and later into the night – actually in the small hours of the morning – until its fading crescent disappears into the sunlight and the time of dark moon is here again. The waning moon can be cupped by a raised, curved left palm in the northern hemisphere and by a right palm in the southern hemisphere.

HOW THE MOON
AFFECTS US

Some, mainly physical, lunar effects are obvious and undeniable while others – often more abstract and therefore harder to quantify or prove – are more difficult to establish with total certainty, causing opinions to differ. Many people simply have a strong 'feeling' that the moon affects us in subtle ways.

EFFECT ON HUMANS

The influence of the moon on human life is far-reaching. Stone Age people regarded the moon and its phases as important, and bones 37,000 years old have been found with notches marking the lunar phases, believed to be the earliest known attempt to record time. The moon was believed to be a god or goddess, a home to deities or mythological creatures, or a place of repose for the spirits of the dead. Barrow mounds were built to face the rising of the moon so that souls could travel upwards on moonbeams.

However, the moon was more than a mere source of myth and enchantment. It was also of great practical use as a marker for the calendar. For instance, the Babylonian month commenced at new moon and the Hebrew calendar was structured around lunar cycles. Even today, the Christian festival of Easter is lunar, falling as it does on the first Sunday after the first full moon following the vernal equinox (the spring day, in the northern hemisphere, when day and night are of equal length). As the moon makes thirteen rounds of the zodiac to a single solar circuit (a year) – with one day to spare – it would seem more sensible to have thirteen months in the year, rather than the twelve months of variable length that we have. Some people believe that the exclusion of lunar measurement from our general calendar reflects a wish to exalt the logical, conscious mind, as often represented by the sun, over the instincts and subconscious, as represented by the moon.

Nonetheless, the importance of the moon is enshrined in our language. The Greek word mene, meaning 'moon', finds its way into English words like dimension, commensurate and many others, showing a recognition of the importance of lunar reckonings – the moon as a measurer and rhythm provider. Menstruation is of course another word with its roots in mene, and one of the closest human links to lunar cycles is seen in the menstrual cycle of women. Even women whose periods do not follow a regular 29-day rhythm find that the moon often causes their periods to come early or late in line with a new or full moon. Some tests have even shown that the light of the full moon can stimulate ovulation, thus aiding fertility.

The word 'lunatic' also comes from a word meaning 'moon' – this time the Latin luna. It was certainly believed that the full moon could cause people to go mad, or increase the dementedness of those already crazy. Today many mental health professionals maintain that the moon really does have an effect on state of mind, and admissions to mental hospitals are said to increase at full moon. Many policemen and women also state that there is a rise in crime at full moon – a claim that is supported by some studies and denied by others. However, lunar effects are, on the whole, extremely hard to measure or prove as they consist of a feeling of disturbance, irrational behaviour or public excitability rather than something that can be quantified, such as an increase in arrests.

Similarly, many midwives claim that they are busier at full moon, although statistics do not consistently support that there are more births at this time. Haemorrhage is also reportedly more common at full moon, meaning this may not be the best time for most types of surgery. And children may be more disruptive than usual during full moon, according to many teachers.

THE TIDES

The tides are a good example of an obvious lunar effect. Galileo denied the influence of the moon on the tides, regarding it as superstition, which proves that even great scientists can make mistakes. In reality, the gravitational pull of the moon accounts for about 70 per cent of the tidal swell, with the sun being responsible for the rest. Spring tides, which are especially high, occur at new and full moon, when the gravitational pull of the sun and moon work together. Neap tides, which are especially low, take place at the first quarter (during the waxing phase) and last quarter (during the waning phase), when the moon is at right angles to the sun.

Our bodies contain water in roughly the same proportion as the earth's oceans. Some people therefore take the view that we must also respond physically to the moon, with our own form of mini 'tides' that account for changes of mood and even changes in our state of health.

EFFECT ON PLANTS AND ANIMALS

Experiments have shown that certain creatures certainly do respond to the moon. Oysters, when brought inland from New Haven, Connecticut and placed in a laboratory in Evanston, Illinois in the 1950s, initially continued to open and close in rhythm with the tides on the beach from whence they had originated. After a while, however, this rhythm altered and it was discovered that the oysters were now directly responding to the passage of the moon overhead in Illinois, hundreds of miles from the ocean. Salmon are also moon-aware: a specific new moon in the northern-hemisphere spring has been proven by scientists to trigger the production of the hormone thyroxin within them, which 'tells'

them to swim inland to reproduce at just the time when they are least likely to be eaten by predators.

Bees have been proven to be most active at new moon, which is appropriate for their function as pollen-carriers as it means they 'deliver' their pollen for fertilization during the waxing moon – a phase of growth and fruition. And conception is most likely to occur in female horses around the time of full moon, even though the oestrus cycle of the horse is, in fact, three weeks.

The water content of plants – which is regulated by the moon – is greatest at full moon. This piece of information even formed the basis of a French law in 1669, which stated that trees could only be felled at the time of the waning moon, because the timber would then be drier and better for its intended purposes. Seeds appear to germinate more quickly if planted just after new moon, growing with the waxing moon; carbohydrate storage in plants is most active around new moon, in preparation for the growth stage associated with the moon's waxing phase; and plant metabolism peaks at full moon – the time associated with many things coming to fruition.

GETTING STARTED WITH MOON ASTROLOGY

Finding out about how the moon affects us requires some thought, mainly because there are two quite distinct factors to consider, as explained earlier – the moon sign and the lunar phases. The moon sign depends on the movement of the moon against the background of stars, while the phase of the moon depends on the position of the moon, relative to the sun in the sky.

THE SKY AS A STAGE

To understand this it can help to imagine yourself in a circular theatre, with the stage all around you. The stage is divided into twelve sections – one for each of the zodiac signs. It is important to remember when considering this that the twelve zodiac signs have a specific order: Aries, Taurus, Gemini, Cancer, Leo, Virgo, Libra, Scorpio, Sagittarius, Capricorn, Aquarius and Pisces. Aries is therefore opposite Libra, and so on, as per the wheel on page 131. Imagine the section that represents Aries – all fiery, with volcanoes and fireworks, and then Taurus, full of green fields and pastures.

Now imagine that there are two dancers on the stage. One is dressed in gold, representing the sun. Another is dressed with silver on the front and black at the back, depicting the moon. The dancers start together in Aries, where you see the black back of the moon dancer – a new moon in Aries. The sun dances slowly through Aries, but the moon skips on into Taurus, Gemini and further. By the time the moon reaches Cancer, she is sideways-on, showing half of her silver side – the moon's first quarter (midway through the waxing phase). On she dances, until by the time she reaches Libra, only her silver front is visible – the full moon. The sun, however, is still in Aries. Now the moon, still dancing against the zodiac backdrop, begins to turn the other way so that you see more of her black back. By the time she is in Capricorn, she is sideways on, half black and half silver – the moon's third quarter (midway through the waning phase). Meanwhile, the sun has been moving so slowly all this time that the moon actually catches up with it just as it moves into Taurus, so the next new moon is in Taurus, the next full moon in Scorpio (one sign after Libra), and so forth.

It is important to note that the influence of each lunar phase extends for three or four days either side of the exact point at which the actual phenomenon occurs, for example, the day of full moon occurs at the middle point of the full moon period, and the phases naturally shade into one another on either side of this. So if you are thinking about planning events in your life according to the phases (see pages 64–129), you will need to judge how to modify what you do to remain in harmony with the moon throughout its transition from one phase to the next. For instance, it might feel right to celebrate and rejoice openly in a relationship at full moon (see pages 56–57), but then switch to being more secluded and inward, reviewing issues and commitments as the moon wanes (see pages 60–61). It is a matter of gentle adjustment. You will also need to think a little about how to blend the advice given for lunar phases (see pages 64–129), with

the guidance for your moon sign (see pages 20–45) and the current moon sign (see pages 78–81, 94–97, 110–113, 126–129). For instance, the energy of an Aries moon could be put into weed-clearing if it is waning, yet might be better spent planting bright or spiky plants if waxing. The aim, however, is that you start to develop an instinctive feel for how the moon phases and signs affect you, so that, with time, your instincts will tell you what feels right to do or not to do.

LUNAR DEPICTIONS

The full moon is represented in charts, diaries and newspapers as a small white disc, while the new moon (or dark moon) is shown as a little black disc. The moon's first quarter (waxing phase), which comes about seven days after new moon, is shown as a half-black half-white disc, and the third quarter (waning phase), which comes about seven days after full moon, is shown in the same way, only with the white half on the other side.

Solar eclipses are shown as a small black disc with a line attached sloping up to the right, and lunar eclipses are shown as two small joined discs. A solar eclipse is usually followed in the same month by a lunar one. Eclipses may mark times of pause, endings or a feeling of emptiness or peace, but they do not have to be negative as they herald a new phase, too. You may feel the effect of eclipses on your emotional life if they occur in your moon sign, or the sign opposite.

WORKING OUT MOON SIGNS

The metaphor of the theatre, shows us that the full moon is always in the sign opposite the sun. So, if the moon looks full, you can find the moon sign simply by noting the current zodiac sign of the sun (most newspapers and magazines have horoscopes that give the dates for these) and counting six signs on from this. New moon always occurs in the same sign as the sun, and newspapers often list this, too. Armed with the knowledge that the moon spends two-and-a-half days in each of the twelve signs of the zodiac, you can then make an intelligent guess as to where the moon may be at the stages in between the full and new moon.

To find the accurate position of the moon at the time of your birth, you would need full planetary tables, or a computer, and because the moon moves so quickly, exact positions for a century would take up far too much space to be printed. Nonetheless, the charts on pages 132–141 reveal your moon sign with 70 per cent exactitude.

Your moon sign will definitely be the sign you find in the chart or the one on either side of it. For example, if the chart shows Sagittarius, your moon sign is 70 per cent likely to be Sagittarius, but it is 100 per cent sure to be Scorpio, Sagittarius or Capricorn. If you feel strongly that you resemble the description of the moon sign next to yours, then you are probably correct. You can find out your precise moon sign by consulting an astrologer.

It is important to realize that you can find the current moon sign by following the same instruction as for your date of birth, but using today's date instead.

Once you have used the charts at the end of this book to work out your moon sign, as well as the current moon sign, you will be armed with two valuable pieces of information that will enable you to gain a deeper understanding of your inner self – as well as the inner self of friends and family, if you so wish.

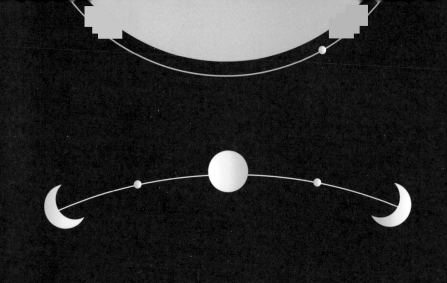

YOUR MOON SIGN

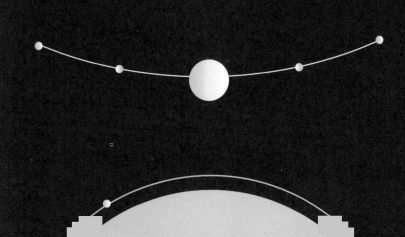

Your moon sign relates to the natural, instinctual parts of you – it is 'where you live'. You may have known your sun sign, or star sign, for many years and may consciously identify with its traits. Just as it is the zodiac sign where the sun was when you were born, your moon sign is the sign that held the moon at your birth. Your sun sign refers to the way you organize yourself, your conscious mind and your ambitions and image. Your moon sign, on the other hand, relates to your subconscious – your habits, emotions, moods and reactions. Like your sun sign, your moon sign is relevant in all areas of life, but while other people may be very aware of your lunar nature, you may not give it much consideration as it is instinctive to you.

Once you have used the charts on pages 132–141 to find your moon sign, the pages in this chapter will allow you to discover the effects that it has on various aspects of your life – mainly emotions, health and beauty, love and relationships, home and garden, and career and finances. Becoming acquainted with how your moon sign influences your character can help to make you a more self-aware and contented person. It can also help you to understand yourself better and realize what you need in life, as well as make you more able to obtain it and therefore lead a more fulfilling, rewarding existence.

YOUR MOON IN
ARIES

EMOTIONS

The moon in Aries is volatile and fiery – you want what you want, and you want it now. And you make no secret of it, as you tend to wear your heart on your sleeve. As a result, you may lose your temper in dramatic fashion when you don't get your own way. Some people tend to be a little wary of you, but those who know you realize they can totally rely on your loyalty and courage. In a crisis you are a wonderful champion, and your energy and determination are an inspiration to the more faint-hearted.

KEYNOTES
- you are impulsive and feisty
- you can be impatient and abrupt
- you act first and think later

HEALTH AND BEAUTY

When you are under stress, you may be especially prone to headaches, as Aries rules the head. If you feel under pressure, release the tension by getting involved in competitive sports or simply by taking a brisk walk. You may be too impatient for a thorough beauty routine, so streamline your grooming with as many two-in-one products as you can. Your hair tends to be hard to tame, so choose an easy-care style that falls into place yet looks striking. You tend to both look and feel good in bright, dramatic colours and outfits that let you move freely.

KEYNOTES
- you are prone to suffering from tension headaches
- vigorous exercise aids relaxation
- your clothes are usually stylish, but comfortable

LOVE AND RELATIONSHIPS

You fall in love at first sight and you may feel very misunderstood if your partner does not comply. However, you need a challenge and you may become disenchanted by a pushover. When it comes to passion, you are given to dramatic gestures, but you also like your freedom. Frank, open and always ready to help, you are happiest when you have a responsive partner who gives you a long leash, but does not let you have everything your own way.

KEYNOTES
- you fall in love fast and hard
- you need a passionate and responsive partner who affords you your independence
- it is best for the relationship if your partner knows when to put his or her foot down

HOME AND GARDEN

You have an 'all-or-nothing' attitude to your domestic setting. You may put great energy into having the best-kept garden and the most immaculate house on the block. Alternatively, you may be so busy that you hardly notice your home. The minimalist look pleases you – it is less fuss and bother, and you like plenty of storage space. In your garden, you like rocks, exotic shrubs and brightly coloured plants. Avoid anything that needs too much attention as you need a garden you can enjoy easily –

somewhere you can go simply to breathe in fresh air.

KEYNOTES
- all-or-nothing approach
- you like simplicity and appreciate a clutter-free environment
- your garden should be easy maintenance

CAREER AND FINANCES

Your ambition and energy need to find outlets in your career. You will never be content stuck in a dull nine-to-five job, so it may suit you to be your own boss. However, you may require someone else to oversee the details. A career as a surgeon, engineer or dynamic salesperson may all appeal, as you continually need fresh challenges. You may spend your money impulsively or, at other times, simply forget that it is even there. Either way, you always want to feel that you know what is going on in terms of finances and employment.

KEYNOTES
- you are dynamic and driven
- being self-employed may suit you best
- it is important for you to feel in control

YOUR MOON IN
TAURUS

EMOTIONS

You are faithful, steady and tolerant, with a slow fuse. Often your physical sensations will put you in touch with your emotions, for instance you get a 'gut feeling'. Although reasonable and placid on the surface, inside you are very much made of animal instinct, and it can take an earthquake – at least! – to make you change. Others find you reliable and kind, but sometimes irritating when you cannot be budged.

KEYNOTES
- you are patient and placid
- you are in tune with your instincts
- routine is very important to you, which can make you stubborn

HEALTH AND BEAUTY

Your calm, laid-back attitude makes for general good health. You enjoy the fine things in life, but sometimes a little too much. This can create problems such as being overweight. However, you are very in tune with your body and will readily take to any fitness regime that makes you feel more physically powerful, especially if it enhances your sex appeal. Steady exercise such as walking will suit you, and once you have established a sensible routine, you will stick to it. When it comes to your looks, you take care of yourself with the best quality beauty products you can find.

KEYNOTES
- your relaxed outlook on life keeps you healthy
- you can be lazy and self-indulgent
- once established, a practical fitness regime is easy for you to maintain

LOVE AND RELATIONSHIPS

In romance you are realistic and tend to settle for something predictable and workable rather than wait for that chorus of violins.

However, if the coup de foudre strikes, you are capable of giving your heart for life and can be very passionate. All you expect in return is affection and stability, although you can be a little possessive. You take great pleasure in making other people comfortable, in physical closeness and in good sex.

KEYNOTES
- your approach to relationships is sensible and practical
- you are capable of lasting love and loyalty
- physical affection is of utmost importance to you

HOME AND GARDEN

A comfortable and secure home is essential to you, and you take great pleasure in ensuring your dwelling is well-equipped. You find nature is a great solace, and you can easily spend many happy hours relaxing in your garden, listening to birdsong. Although too-relaxed to be a perfectionist, your thorough approach is apparent in well-managed surroundings. Your artistic flair comes out in your impeccable taste in colours and ornaments.

KEYNOTES
- a safe and loving home is of paramount importance to you
- your surroundings are both extremely comfortable and highly tasteful
- you love spending time in nature as you find it nourishing for the soul

CAREER AND FINANCES

Money, to you, is a matter of common sense, and you keep accounts smoothly and naturally. Occasionally you may be extravagant over something very beautiful or pleasurable, but you soon re-balance the books. Hands-on or artistic careers may appeal, or a financial job. You may find yourself in a position of responsibility almost by accident, but once there, you discharge your responsibilities thoroughly.

KEYNOTES
- you are naturally sensible with money, but allow yourself the occasional extravagance
- you may be drawn to practical careers, involving your hands, or a job in finance
- success often comes with little obvious effort

YOUR MOON IN
GEMINI

EMOTIONS

Your Gemini moon puts you at a slight distance from your emotions because you are always analysing and weighing things up. You are afraid of getting carried away and losing all sense and reason. Others find you rather cool and controlled, but they value your ability to shed fresh light on their problems, and your detached, yet lively approach is refreshing and reassuring. Freedom is very important to you, and variety is essential.

KEYNOTES
- you analyse your emotions
- your head tends to rule your heart
- a sense of independence and perpetual forward movement are essential to you in life

HEALTH AND BEAUTY

The fact that you sometimes deny or bottle up your feelings can render you sick with stress, as you try to make sense of what you could just allow yourself to feel. Talking is wonderful therapy for you, so make sure you have plenty of sympathetic friends, or even have counselling sessions. You are a great fidget, which tends to ensure that you remain slender and fit. You are capable of keeping to a sensible schedule and beauty routine, but make sure that it has some built-in variety for you are very easily bored.

KEYNOTES
- stress can result if you repress your feelings
- it is important that you talk about your innermost emotions
- you tend to look very young for your age

LOVE AND RELATIONSHIPS

You need a partner who is a good listener, for you chatter incessantly. You can be very quick-witted and entertaining, and mental stimulation is essential to you in any relationship. You can be an incorrigible flirt and may make sure that you have a second string to your bow until you really feel you have found the right person for you. When that happens you will choose with your head as well as your heart, and it may take you a while to commit. Your partner should share your tastes in books and theatre, and be able to surprise you on occasion.

KEYNOTES
- you need a partner willing – and able – to listen to your endless chatter
- flirty and mischievous, it takes you a while to commit to someone
- a mental rapport with your partner is essential, as is an element of fun

HOME AND GARDEN

All DIY projects you take on board should be quick to complete as you get bored easily. You need plenty of space in your home for your books, magazines and all the latest information and communication technology. Your garden should be low maintenance, preferably with colourful shrubs that flower at different times of the year, to give you perpetual variety and colour. Friends are essential to you, so

you will prefer your living area to accommodate guests. You like to re-organize the furniture regularly.

KEYNOTES
- you prefer to be in light, modern surroundings
- it is essential for you to keep in touch with what's going on in the world
- you like to make changes as often as possible

CAREER AND FINANCES

You are very good with words, which means that a career in publishing or in the media might suit you. Whatever you do needs to have plenty of variety, preferably with chances to meet new people every day and to travel a lot. You are resourceful in managing your finances, and because you keep a cool head you are not too often tempted to extravagance, although you may treat yourself to a last-minute holiday if life gets boring.

KEYNOTES
- a career in publishing or the media might suit your strengths
- you enjoy meeting new people
- you keep a cool head with your money but may spend impulsively on holidays and trips

YOUR MOON IN
CANCER

HEALTH AND BEAUTY

It is very important for you to feel nurtured. If you do not feel emotionally 'fed', the danger is you may fall into the bad habit of craving sweet food or alcohol, which could damage your health slowly and surely, without you even knowing. Your moods affect how you look – one day you may be very well-dressed and the next, you may decide just to put on any old comfortable thing. You find long, hot baths particularly soothing. When your imagination is working negatively you may be prone to vague fears; positive thinking and sensible habits will keep you smiling.

KEYNOTES
- emotional upsets can affect your digestion
- your moods affect the way you look
- your imagination needs to be positively channelled or you may become fearful

LOVE AND RELATIONSHIPS

Being a true romantic, you thrive on hearts and flowers and long to feel you 'belong'. When you care

EMOTIONS

Your emotions run very deep, which makes you a motherly person (regardless of sex), for whom it is very important to feel needed. As you are very imaginative, you need to be careful to keep your feet on the ground by being with people who support you. Being a sensitive, moody soul, you may fear rejection, so can sometimes be manipulative. Your dreams are central to your life.

KEYNOTES
- you are a deeply emotional person who likes to mother people
- imaginative and artistic, you need to keep your feet on the ground
- your extreme sensitivity can, at times, lead you to manipulate others

for someone, you love to look out for all their creature comforts and you are very sensitive to their every mood and need. However, you can be quite easily hurt and will then close off inside your crab's shell, and it may take much coaxing to bring you out. You are likely to want to have children, but if this isn't possible, then you will want to share deep creativity in some other way with your partner.

KEYNOTES
- you are sensitive to your partner's every need
- your sensitivity means you can be easily hurt
- family and security are high priorities

HOME AND GARDEN

You are a true home-maker, and a domestic situation brings out the best of your talents. You may favour traditional decor, with plenty of photos, nooks and crannies for ornaments and grandma's heirlooms, as well as a special place for the family cat. You have trouble parting with anything, so may well be surrounded by clutter. Your garden flourishes under your loving attention and you take special pleasure in growing

vegetables, as you enjoy cooking for friends and family.

KEYNOTES
- you are a traditional home-maker
- tidiness is difficult for you because you tend to hoard things
- you love your garden and have a natural flair for tending to it

CAREER AND FINANCES

Financial security is crucial to you, and you like to have proper plans in place for savings, pensions and insurance. You budget and prioritize instinctively, but you may be tempted to buy more than you should for your children and loved ones. You are likely to be happiest in the caring professions, such as medicine, social work or some branches of police work. You do not like changing jobs, but will certainly leave if the atmosphere is unhappy.

KEYNOTES
- financial security is a priority
- the caring professions appeal to you
- you prefer to stay in one job, but will leave if your colleagues are uncaring or unfriendly towards you

YOUR MOON IN
LEO

EMOTIONS

Your fiery Leo moon makes you a flamboyant and dramatic person. You are generous to a fault and people experience you as warm-hearted and cheerful. However, you are readily upset by anything that offends your sense of 'special-ness' and when this happens, everyone around you will know all about it! Everything about you is larger than life, especially your emotions. This means that you may be easily hurt, but, thankfully, you soon get back on your feet.

KEYNOTES
- you are warm-hearted and extravagant
- when you aren't made to feel special you become very upset
- you are easily hurt but soon bounce back

HEALTH AND BEAUTY

Leo rules the heart, and the chances are you have a good colour to your skin and lots of enthusiasm to put into exercise. You are competitive and like to be seen as a leader and winner. It is important for your health that you release any emotional pain you feel, so that your heart can truly heal. Massage is very soothing for you, making you feel like purring, like the big Leo cat you are! And the freedom to just relax, have fun and be playful is also important to your health. With regard to your appearance, only the best will do and you love designer labels.

KEYNOTES
- you are enthusiastic and competitive
- massage will help to release any emotional blockages you may have
- you have the highest of standards

LOVE AND RELATIONSHIPS

You do everything in a big way, and falling in love is no exception. Your partner may be deluged with expensive gifts, and wined and dined to distraction! If things go wrong, your grief can be overwhelming, but if your friends rally round, you soon bounce back. In an established relationship you can be quite demanding because you expect the same high standards in a partner as you do in anything else. When you are happy, you are capable of total devotion and commitment.

KEYNOTES
- you fall in love dramatically and deeply
- you are a great one for the extravagant gesture
- once committed, you are 100 per cent dedicated and expect the same in return

HOME AND GARDEN

You don't like doing housework or gardening, yet you like your home to look sumptuous, and your garden to be lush and the envy of all the neighbours. You will probably employ someone to help with the chores, if you can. Your taste is impressive, and you spare no expense making sure everything co-ordinates. You love to entertain, to show off your home and to have fun with friends. It is important to you that your surroundings shout

'success' so space for trophies is essential!

KEYNOTES
- you like a home and garden to be proud of
- chores do not appeal and you will get hired help if possible
- entertaining is a 'must' so your home needs space for this

CAREER AND FINANCES

Your job needs to make you feel important. Management roles suit you as you are creative, you are able to see the total picture, you can make decisions based on intuition and you can hold your own. In your career, as in all else, you like to excel and be admired. With money you are torn two ways as it hurts your pride to be in debt, yet you often get carried away with extravagant purchases. The answer is a large income – which you usually achieve.

KEYNOTES
- you need to feel valued in your career
- you have managerial talent and are very creative
- you need a large salary to meet your needs

YOUR MOON IN
VIRGO

EMOTIONS

With your Virgo moon, being in control of your emotions is very important to you, and you may come across as cool and reserved. You are practical and serious, tending to analyse your feelings, until thinking about how you feel distances you from the actual experience of the emotions themselves. You do not like to expose yourself, fearing hurt or criticism, so you only express what you feel in a restrained manner. Your refinement and common sense can be very reassuring to others.

KEYNOTES
- you need to feel in control of your emotions
- you usually analyse your emotions rather than just feel them
- you may be shy but others appreciate your good sense

HEALTH AND BEAUTY

Your digestive system is easily upset by any form of stress, so you need to be relaxed and happy while you eat. Tension headaches are also likely, as you worry about details. Relaxation techniques such as yoga, where there is a physical element to what you are doing, will be of great benefit as they appeal to your down-to-earth approach to life. You are supremely health-conscious, which includes being careful about what you eat. Your appearance is faultless, as you are very fastidious about grooming.

KEYNOTES
- you tend to be smartly dressed and groomed
- stress can make you ill, but physical-based therapies help
- you tend to be careful about eating healthy food

LOVE AND RELATIONSHIPS

Helping others will make you feel worthwhile, but sometimes you take on too much and find yourself dragged down by other people's problems. You do not readily give your heart, needing to weigh things up carefully before getting involved. You need lots of reassurance from those you love, but you are realistic about what to expect in relationships. Though you are not the most passionate lover in the zodiac, you enjoy physical closeness and appreciate a touch or hug from a loved one.

KEYNOTES
- you have a natural instinct for helping others
- you are cautious about bestowing love and trust
- you tend to be practical rather than sentimental

HOME AND GARDEN

Your flair for organization is evident in your home. Your living space is tidy to a fault, as being surrounded by mess upsets you. A secret to your neat home is that when you are under stress you make yourself busy with the duster or have a big sort-out of your closets. Your garden also benefits from your painstaking care, and you may have a penchant for growing herbs for medicine and cooking. Weeds have no chance when you're on the job and your natural talent in the garden means your plants thrive. Because you are in tune with nature, walks in the country will soothe you greatly.

KEYNOTES
- you are well-organized to a fault
- you are impeccably clean and tidy
- you are in tune with nature and have a talent for growing things

CAREER AND FINANCES

Your intelligence and precision point you towards a career in technology or engineering, though you may also be a wonderful scientific or medical researcher. You are clever and methodical at work and find it easy to concentrate, working diligently and systematically. You are careful with money and make wise, safe investments. Your high standards and knack for organization keep your business affairs in good order and your projects on schedule.

KEYNOTES
- you can be a workaholic
- you are happiest when being useful and productive
- your standards are of the highest quality

EMOTIONS

Harmony and beautiful surroundings are essential to you, and you tend to charm everyone you meet. It is important to you to please people, and your calm presence is very soothing. You can't bear disagreements, although you do like to have the chance to air your views. Sometimes you just can't make up your mind. Although you may appear responsive, you are quite emotionally cool because internal balance must be maintained.

KEYNOTES
- a calm atmosphere is essential to you
- it is hard for you to make up your mind
- you use charm to get your own way

HEALTH AND BEAUTY

It is important for your health that you are surrounded by beauty and a pleasant atmosphere; living with strife can make you ill. You can be a little lazy, love chocolates and treats, and you tend not to have great self-discipline. For you to exercise there needs to be some pleasure built in, so you are often happiest doing it with a friend. Looking good is vital to you and you may take a long time choosing clothes and grooming yourself.

KEYNOTES
- unpleasantness is bad for your health
- you may be lazy and indulge in treats
- looking good is a 'must'

LOVE AND RELATIONSHIPS

You know just how to draw other people in with your charm and will have plenty of opportunities for romance. In fact you have an instinctive talent for the whole 'love thing'. You may lose sight of your own preferences in your efforts to please others though, and you only feel truly at home when with a special someone. However, you will want to be able to discuss the relationship in a civilized manner. Getting on well with each other is more important to you than steamy passion, so you need someone who shares your tastes.

KEYNOTES
- you have a natural flair for romance
- your own personality may become absorbed in your lover's
- being able to talk openly with each other is more your style than grand passion

HOME AND GARDEN

You have a talent for interior decor and create a lovely ambience. You are not fond of living alone but, in the end, prefer that to living with disagreements. Housework is not your style, and you would far rather paint a wall than get out the vacuum cleaner. Muddle can be tolerated as long as it consists of beautiful things – in any case you may find it quite hard to decide what to throw out! In your garden, you love flowers and maybe a tasteful statue or two.

KEYNOTES
- beautiful surroundings are a 'must'
- you prefer not to live alone
- flowers and music are your passions

CAREER AND FINANCES

Your flair for diplomacy could find expression in a legal profession, counselling or mediation. Alternatively, careers in art or music may afford expression for your talents. Either way, you have expensive tastes, so your salary needs to be high to accommodate them! Not being fond of hard work, you need to find a niche where charm will work for you. You are tolerant to a fault, but nonetheless you will become distressed by unfairness – towards your colleagues as much as towards yourself. Managing money is not your strong point, for you can never resist something beautiful!

KEYNOTES
- diplomatic or artistic careers may suit equally
- one thing you cannot bear is unfairness
- managing money is not your strong point, but somehow you win out

YOUR MOON IN
SCORPIO

EMOTIONS

Your feelings are very strong indeed, so much so that you may be almost fearful of their intensity. Because of this you tend to keep them to yourself, rather than let others see your vulnerability. You like to know other people's secrets, so that you can be one step ahead. You can be manipulative and even spiteful sometimes, and you never forget an insult or slight. However, you are intensely loyal and very courageous.

KEYNOTES
- your emotions are extremely powerful
- you can be secretive and manipulative
- your bravery and loyalty are second to none

HEALTH AND BEAUTY

For you, a loving and fulfilling sex life makes for maximum health. You have a tendency to become obsessive, so it is very important to direct this into something positive, like deep study, rather than letting your imagination work overtime. You may be radical about diet and exercise, almost punishing your body, but sometimes you may relapse into self-destruct with comfort eating and no exercise at all. Cleansing therapies like colonic hydrotherapy may appeal to you, and you may even consider cosmetic surgery if displeased with your looks.

KEYNOTES
- a good sex life keeps you at your best
- your intensity needs positive direction
- radical regimes and therapies may suit you

LOVE AND RELATIONSHIPS

You are an extremely passionate person and when you fall in love it is 'truly, madly, deeply'. However, you may not express this and you may try to control the person you love in any way you can, rather than risk being hurt. You are capable of being very suspicious and jealous – in fact often you look so hard for trouble that you inevitably find it. However, you are an exciting and magnetic individual, and once you find someone who can love you the way you need to be loved – completely – then there is no-one more caring and supportive.

KEYNOTES
- you are very passionate and expect a lot from your lover
- jealousy and suspicion can be problematic
- once you have found the right person, you are deeply committed

HOME AND GARDEN

You insist on privacy in your home so may prefer thick curtains, the protection of a hedge or fence, burglar alarms or a large security dog. You like to have regular clear-outs, although you retain family photos and mementoes. You work hard in your garden and have a personal vendetta with any weeds. If possible you may like to have a pond for its calming quality. Your garden should be a haven, where you can soothe your soul surrounded by peace and greenery.

KEYNOTES
- privacy is essential to you
- regular clear-outs ensure you retain control
- your garden is your refuge

CAREER AND FINANCES

The superficial does not satisfy you in anything, and you need to feel that your work is in some way crucial. You may be attracted to surgery, medicine, the armed forces or the police. Often you work behind the scenes but wield a lot of power. You like to keep control of your finances, like all else, and you are likely to be very self-disciplined with your spending. You will want the protection of more-than-adequate insurance.

KEYNOTES
- you need a career that is deep, meaningful and challenging
- usually you achieve a position of power behind the scenes
- your finances are well-controlled

YOUR MOON IN
SAGITTARIUS

EMOTIONS

Generally upbeat and optimistic, you like to see the bright side to everything and you have a very lively sense of humour. Your emotions are extravagant, and you tend to swing between hope and despair, but inevitably end up smiling. A great philosopher, you like to look for the true meaning of life. Freedom is essential to you, for you need to explore and experience. You can be casual, off-hand and unreliable, but you are generous and warm-hearted, so most of the time you are forgiven!

KEYNOTES
- cheerful and humorous, you are fun to be with
- you can be a person of extremes
- people forgive your unreliability because of your generosity of spirit

HEALTH AND BEAUTY

Believing you are indestructible, you often take on far too much and run yourself ragged trying to keep promises. You need to slow down with some form of meditation, and regular walking makes you feel powerful and alive. In your beauty care you expect a lot of yourself, and you may surround yourself with lots of expensive creams and potions. Sometimes you over-indulge, but – although you have little patience with diets – your high energy usually ensures that you keep slim.

KEYNOTES
- you take on too much and need to slow down
- you spend a lot on beauty care but may be too impatient to use it
- being constantly on the go keeps you slim

LOVE AND RELATIONSHIPS

With you, there are no half measures – you throw yourself whole-heartedly into relationships, turning your partner into a god or goddess. It can hit you hard when you find out that they are mortal after all, and you may fall out of love just as quickly as you fall in love. Openness and honesty are important to you – in fact, at times, you can be too honest, but at least people know where they stand. Your relationship is cemented by shared plans for the future, and nothing is too much trouble when you truly love.

KEYNOTES
- you can fall both in and out of love quickly
- your partner should share your passion for adventure
- sincerity and integrity are vital to you

HOME AND GARDEN

You like a home you can show off to all your friends and you like plenty of space. A panoramic view does wonders for you, as does a touch of luxury and the exotic. You prefer rich colours and fabrics and you hate locks, so the back door is always open to your garden – which should be as large as possible, with plenty of objects of interest, such as statues and unusual plants. Games suit your playful nature, so a swing, trampoline or tennis court would suit.

KEYNOTES
- a home with a beautiful view is your style
- space and openness is essential
- it is important for you to have somewhere to express your playful side

CAREER AND FINANCES

You are the last of the big spenders, relying on a lucky break to get you through – which it usually does! You tend to gamble and often win. Being an opportunist, you have an eye for the best bargains and the most lucrative investments. You may be best self-employed, as an entrepreneur or salesperson, for this gives you the freedom and scope that you need. However, because you are far-seeing, you may be drawn into philosophy, law, teaching or some form of spiritual work.

KEYNOTES
- you are extravagant but your opportunism brings great gains
- being self-employed gives you the independence and flexibility you need
- you are drawn towards both spiritual and intellectual pursuits

YOUR MOON IN
CAPRICORN

EMOTIONS

Self-sufficiency is all-important to you, and you rarely give away much about yourself. Often you like to be alone and you find your security in your surroundings rather than in other people. You are totally controlled and unflappable and others may experience you as cold, until they hit trouble. Then you offer practical help that is hard to beat and a steady, reassuring presence. You have a sentimental streak and are very kind, as long as your boundaries are respected.

KEYNOTES
- being self-sufficient, you are often happiest alone
- your constant composure can make you come across as cool
- you are happy to help people in need on a practical level

HEALTH AND BEAUTY

Tension can make you stiff, so you need flowing exercise such as t'ai chi to loosen you up. If you repress your feelings, they may raise their heads as colds and flu, so it is worth admitting – at least to yourself – how you feel. If you are well-balanced, your skin will be flawless; break-outs reveal inner hurts. You are more than capable of keeping to a sensible regime when it comes to exercise, eating and beauty care, but you may need to remind yourself that you are worth the effort.

KEYNOTES
- tension can be released by flowing exercise
- you are good at keeping to healthy routines
- your self-esteem may be low, so you need an occasional boost

LOVE AND RELATIONSHIPS

It is not easy for you to give your heart, and even when you do it can be hard for you to trust. Being a pessimist, you are looking for drawbacks all the time. This can make you appear critical and judgemental, which in turn, can bring about the very thing you fear most: rejection. When you meet someone who is right for you, you make their lives really secure and comfortable and you are always there with a big hug and a cup of tea even if you do not know what to say.

KEYNOTES

- being naturally pessimistic, you find it hard to trust
- you fear rejection, and so may reject others without meaning to
- once you find the right partner you are a tower of strength

HOME AND GARDEN

Your home is your castle, where you like to feel safe and private. Because you like to be prepared for anything, your home may be full of gadgets. Although you prize organization you are unlikely to be tidy because you hate throwing anything out – you prefer to hang on to all reminders of the past, from dusty albums to great-grandma's sewing machine. Your garden should preferably be walled and private. You are not fond of changes, so even the familiar weeds may remain!

KEYNOTES

- you need your home to feel secure and private
- gadgets and memorabilia abound
- a traditional garden appeals to you

CAREER AND FINANCES

Your job is all-important – and can take up too much of your time. Your talent for routine and organization makes you an excellent administrator or manager, but you may also enjoy hands-on, practical work in building or farming. Work with antiques and archives may also appeal. You keep a tight rein on your budget, making long-term investments that tie up your money for many years, as you have plenty of patience. You keep your eye on the clock and your assignments on schedule at all times.

KEYNOTES

- you can be a workaholic
- administrative, management or practical roles may satisfy
- you are very aware of the passage of time and make long-term investments

YOUR MOON IN
AQUARIUS

EMOTIONS

You are calm and detached, and often have a quirky take on things. Strong emotions are not your style so they may make you uncomfortable. However, you can be very wise and philosophical about human nature. You love your freedom, and while a crowd of friends is important to you, there is always something inaccessible about you. You can see many sides to things and are generally broad-minded but this can mean that, at times, you forget the smaller, practical things in life.

KEYNOTES
- you are an individual, with strong ideals
- although you enjoy spending time with other people, you don't like to get too close to them
- you are great at viewing the bigger picture but sometimes you can lose sight of the details in the process

HEALTH AND BEAUTY

You love the outdoors and probably have a fresh, healthy complexion. When it comes to clothes and make-up, fuss and bother is not your style – you prefer a natural look. Pure, organic food, fresh fruit and vegetables all appeal to you, and you have good self-discipline. You like to try unusual diets, new theories on health and fitness interest you and a high-tech gym may inspire you. Unusual or new sports can appeal and you are a good team player as long as you can make a unique contribution.

KEYNOTES
- you love simplicity and being outdoors suits you
- you are self-disciplined
- new theories on health and fitness fascinate you

LOVE AND RELATIONSHIPS

When it comes to love, you can be quite a shy person. Despite the fact that you understand a lot about it in theory, it is often hard for you to cope with the reality of emotional demands. An abiding friendship is likely to mean more to you than anything steamier. Relationships that are in some way different from the norm may also appeal to you, such as those brought about by communal living. Honesty and openness are vital to you, and when you do settle for one person, it is for a meeting of minds.

KEYNOTES
- alternative living arrangements may appeal as you delay committing
- honesty and mental rapport are your priorities in a partnership

HOME AND GARDEN

You love breathing in fresh air, so large windows are essential in your home to let in plenty of light. You prefer an uncluttered look, with state-of-the-art technology – including the latest television, sound system and computer. Visitors to your home are likely to be surprised by your highly individual taste, maybe by pictures on the ceiling or strangely angled lighting, for example. You may choose to have a wild garden, or create within it a haven for endangered species. Your home and garden are always open house to friends.

KEYNOTES
- you like to keep up-to-date with the latest in technology
- your home is modern, striking, individual and unusual

CAREER AND FINANCES

Money-making is of no great concern to you, yet, often, you find that money accumulates while you are busy doing something else. You want to do great things for the world, so your career is likely to involve conservation or charitable concerns. Alternatively, you may like to work outdoors, for example, as a park warden. Big spending does not appeal to you, and you probably prefer to shop second-hand and take part in community schemes. You seek out ethical investments and banking, and probably give regularly to charity.

KEYNOTES
- your ideals are more important to you than money-making
- work may involve charity, the environment or animals, and you like to be outdoors
- alternative economies such as community schemes appeal to you

YOUR MOON IN
PISCES

EMOTIONS

You are a real dreamer and may spend your life longing for a fairytale. You feel so many things that you may be confused and find it hard to make up your mind about what you really want. Your imagination is very powerful, so you are likely either to be very unrealistic or quite pragmatic and self-centred. You are deeply sympathetic, feeling the hurts of the world as if they were your own, and have powerful intuitions.

KEYNOTES

- your dreams are paramount to your existence
- you often experience conflicting emotions, which can make you feel confused
- intuitive and sympathetic, you tend to attract the needy

HEALTH AND BEAUTY

Routines of any sort make you miserable, and the very idea of a diet makes you yearn to eat all the wrong things. You have a sweet tooth and may over-indulge in alcohol, especially when things get tough. Swimming and gentle exercise in pleasant surroundings suits your sensitive spirit. Dancing may inspire you and time laughing with friends can keep at bay the depression to which you can be prone. You try many different beauty approaches, hoping for miracles, but usually end up using the products that simply 'seem nice'.

KEYNOTES

- you do not adapt easily to routine
- sweets and alcohol may tempt you
- dancing, swimming and simply laughing can enhance your life

LOVE AND RELATIONSHIPS

To you, life without love is nothing. Romantic and imaginative, you are often in a dream of hearts and flowers or in a switched-off state that protects you from life's setbacks. You put your lover on a pedestal and may start to value their feelings and wishes as more important than your own. You are a charming individual with an intuitive way of giving other people what they want. The down side of this is that you may manipulate others in the process.

KEYNOTES
- you are extremely romantic
- you may well sacrifice your own wishes to meet those of your partner
- you are charming and intuitive, yet you can also be manipulative

HOME AND GARDEN

The ambience in your home should be as enchanting and ethereal as possible, with crystals, floating voile and maybe a large fish tank. With decor, as with all else, it may be hard for you to make up your mind, and reality may disappoint, in comparison to your visions. This means that you make frequent changes in your surroundings. Your garden should have a hint of magic, with a water feature, exotic plants and well-chosen statues. Because you often feel tired, a hammock or a comfortable chair in the shade are ideal for relaxing.

KEYNOTES
- an almost magical ambience appeals to you, but reality often disappoints you, so you make constant changes
- you like to relax in the shade of your garden

CAREER AND FINANCES

Money confuses you and the thought of working for a living fills you with exhaustion. However, you are resilient and resourceful and have a talent for survival. You may have special gifts for music, drama or art, which can make you surprising sums of money. Alternatively, you may be in the healing professions. You do not like to be in the same job for too long, unless it is a vocation. You have an intuitive feeling for the right investments and for getting help from people.

KEYNOTES
- working full-time and organizing your finances can seem overwhelming to you
- your natural talents may earn you money
- your intuition helps you with financial decisions

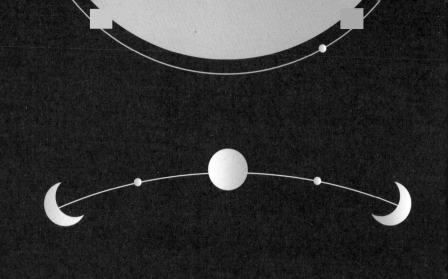

THE PHASES OF
THE MOON

In the following pages we explain the meanings of the four phases of the moon, so that you can become attuned to the lunar rhythms and begin to relate them to your life. Once armed with this knowledge, you will start to notice the effect of the moon on your moods and feelings, and you may also choose to mark each of the moon's phases with certain, relevant activities.

It is a good idea to start a lunar diary where you can make a note of all your fluctuations of mood and temperament in connection with the moon's phases. For instance, you may notice that your energy levels are higher during certain periods; that you are more emotional on some days and more creative on others; that you feel like eating or sleeping more on certain days; or that your sex drive goes up or down. Why not make a note of your dreams in a separate diary too?

It is also useful to set aside a small 'lunar observance' area in your home, or 'moon altar', where you can place things that remind you of the phases, such as candles, ornaments, cards, crystals or whatever else appeals to you. Specific suggestions will be given in the appropriate sections.

DARK MOON — NEW MOON

Dark moon is when there is no moon visible in the sky (see page 12). It is a period of inwardness, retreat and meditation. It relates to endings, but also to beginnings, for a new cycle is unfolding as the moon separates from the sun, forming a graceful, shining curve in the evening sky – the new moon. The dark–new moon phase offers a good opportunity to examine the things in your life that are, or need to be, coming to an end, or at least to a point of fundamental change.

It is a time to review your relationships – to look into your heart and try to be honest about what is working for you and what is not. For instance, are you hanging on to a relationship out of habit or because you fear change? Likewise in respect of your career – is it going the way you want or do you feel as if you are on a treadmill? What about your home? Are there problems that you are ignoring, either in respect of your emotions or more practical factors, like decor and appliances? It can also be useful to try to explore whether you are trapped in any psychological patterns from childhood, such as dependency or a need to please others. If there are metaphorical weeds of any sort in your life, now is the time to

remove them and to plant new seeds. You can start by making a note of these in your lunar diary.

MYTH AND LEGEND

Such ideas of endings and rebirth are depicted in mythology worldwide, as ancient peoples saw heavenly cycles as signs of immortality. The Maori people of New Zealand, for example, believe that there is a magical land beyond the clouds, or lost in the mists of the horizon. This is called 'the land of the water of life of the gods'. In this wonderful place is an enchanted lake, known as the living water of Kane, which possesses the power to bring the dead to life. The Maori believe that the moon dies at the end of its cycle and returns to this lake, where the living water brings it back to life and sets it on course again. Such legends encourage us to recognize and accept the moon's cycles of death and rebirth, which can be very therapeutic. You might like to consider some of the endings that you have experienced in light of this, such as the end of a relationship, the death of a pet or the loss of a job. Did any such event turn out to hold the seeds of a new beginning? For instance, did the end of your relationship herald a new independent phase in your life? Did losing your pet teach you something positive about life? Or did the freedom of unemployment lead anywhere productive? If not, could there be a way for this to happen? Record your thoughts in your lunar journal.

LOOK WITHIN YOURSELF

As the dark–new lunar phase is all about slowing down and looking within, you should choose objects for your moon altar (the space in your home dedicated to the moon and its effect on you) that help you to do these things. You might choose dark blue, purple or black candles as these colours seem fitting for the 'dark' moon. Crystals such as onyx, obsidian or apache tears would also be suitable, as well as figures of nocturnal creatures such as owls, which represent wisdom, and flowers

such as violets and purple pansies. Pictures or postcards that evoke mystery to you are also good, and anything personal that reminds you of endings and fresh starts in your life can join them. You may also like to look up the exact time of new moon and light a small silver candle to celebrate the start of this new beginning.

DARK MOON EXERCISE FOR SELF-DEVELOPMENT

In the hustle and bustle of life it is easy to be carried relentlessly onwards, never making the time to reflect and actually decide what changes you would like to make. Dark moon is a time of stillness, so take this opportunity to attune to the calm and peace of the moon, to listen to your inner voice and to take charge of your life as a new cycle commences. The actions in the exercise below are symbolic, so are effective in getting through to your subconscious mind, which is where new starts truly begin.

WHAT YOU WILL NEED

- relaxing music
- a black scarf
- a black candle
- a piece of scrap paper
- a pen
- a white candle
- your lunar journal
- a silver-inked pen
- a box of matches
- a heat-proof container
- a seed (such as a sunflower seed)
- a small pot of compost

WHAT TO DO

1 Light the black candle and sit comfortably with the black scarf over your shoulders, looking at the flame and listening to your music. Let images flow through your mind of what you would like to let go of in your life. Allow any feelings associated with this to come to the surface. What three main things need to end?

2 When you feel sure, write down the three items you would like to banish from your life – with an ordinary pen on a scrap of paper. Twist the paper into a taper and light it in the candle flame. Then place it in the heatproof dish, say a firm goodbye to it all and watch it burn away.

3 Now use the black candle to light the white one – representing all things new and pure – and allow yourself some time to reflect on new ventures, intentions or qualities that you would like to introduce into your life.

4 Once your thoughts have clarified, write down the three things you would like to pursue, this time in your lunar journal, using a silver pen. Still listening to your music, imagine clearly how life will be when you make these changes and decorate your page with drawings, if you feel like it. Spend as long as you like in this visualizing and planning phase.

5 Now take the seed between your palms and repeat your intentions. Say 'I plant this seed at new moon. It is the seed of ... (name your resolutions). As the moon grows in the sky, so will ... (my resolutions) grow in my life'. Push the seed into the compost in your pot, making sure it is well bedded-in.

6 Place the pot somewhere suitable and water your seed, moderately, as the moon waxes. If it does not germinate, don't worry – you can plant another.

7 Get in the habit of visualizing your fresh intentions and spinning out scenarios of the new you – especially before you go to sleep each night and in the morning when you wake up. It is a good idea to place a small reminder by the bed to help you to do this. Soon, the changes will become a reality in your life, and you can build on them with each new moon.

8 With your resolutions safely recorded in your diary, you can take it out again at the next new moon and reflect upon it. Have your intentions changed? If so, make a note of why, along with all the thought processes that have gone with this change, for this is your own cycle of endings and beginnings. You can make new resolutions or you can simply re-affirm your previous decisions at each dark moon.

WAXING MOON

Waxing moon is a time of growth and expansion, as the slender crescent fills out, becoming closer and closer in shape to a sphere. When does new moon become waxing moon? There is no strict demarcation for the phases – when you first see the new moon, the waxing period is already getting under way. The phases all blend into one another, so it's best to trust and go by how you feel.

With the waxing moon you may feel your energies increase and you are likely to wish to make fresh starts. A new creative project, hitherto just an idea, may begin to blossom into something productive. You now have the determination to start a new exercise regime or diet, to begin decorating at home or to tackle a difficult project at work. All things seem possible, and you are likely to feel that there are many options in life.

It is a good idea to spend time with children, young people and kittens or puppies at this time, for they are likely to inspire in you the faith in the future that will ensure you get maximum benefit from this phase. Also make cakes or bread, watch them rise and as

you eat them, or serve them to your family, visualize abundance coming into your lives.

This time of increase can also be used to encourage your finances to grow. An exercise to encourage this involves standing on grass, looking at the moon in the evening sky (preferably not through glass), turning over the silver in your pocket or purse and imagining your bank account swelling. Finish by bowing three times to the waxing moon and making a wish.

SIGNS OF GROWTH

Think about all the things in your life that are growing, and write about them in your lunar journal. Go outdoors into nature and look for signs of growth. Even if it is winter, there will be something to inspire you, such as a swelling stream or a drift of beautiful white snow. Bring anything appealing home with you for your altar and record all your feelings and experiences in your journal.

POSITIVE ACTION

The things you choose for your moon altar during the waxing phase should be reminders of growing energy, enterprise and activity. White or silver candles, signifying freshness, are suitable. Useful crystals might include blue lace agate, aventurine, turquoise or any other stone that you feel encourages clarity and positive action. Flowers might be daisies, hyacinths, jasmine, lily-of-the-valley or any others to which you feel drawn. Swift-moving animals such as rabbits, or white birds such as doves, convey the innocence of the time. Pictures that remind you of adventure, excitement and creativity, and anything personal that you find stimulating and invigorating can join them.

THE MAIDEN GODDESS

The waxing, full and waning phases of the moon have been linked respectively to the three elements of the Triple Goddess: Maiden, Mother and Crone, which relate to the three corresponding stages in life – the innocence of youth, the maturity and fertility of the middle years and the wisdom of old age. One well-known 'maiden' goddess was the Greek goddess Artemis. She was the divine huntress, who guarded her freedom fiercely. Legend told how she would set loose her hounds on any man bold enough to spy on her in the forest. If you wish for self-assertion and the courage to take hold of your own destiny, then Artemis, or any hunter/huntress figure may be appropriate for your waxing moon altar. Similarly, any statue of a youth or maiden that signifies freshness and vitality would be appropriate for waxing moon exercise.

WAXING MOON EXERCISE
FOR CREATIVITY

As the moon waxes, so energy and opportunities seem to increase. The waxing phase is therefore a good time to boost your productivity and creativity in tune with the moon. Think about which of your activities or projects you would like to move forward – this might be your work, a hobby, something artistic, a community or family matter, or anything else that is important to you. It is best to focus on just one project each lunar month, or you may find that you simply become too busy.

WHAT YOU WILL NEED
- plenty of pieces of modelling clay in a colour or colours of your choice
- a thick white ribbon
- pins with different coloured heads
- a white candle
- rosemary oil (see below), diluted in a carrier oil such as grapeseed (one drop of oil to one teaspoon of carrier)

ROSEMARY OIL CAUTION
Cleansing and stimulating rosemary oil traditionally aids remembrance and clarity of mind. However, it should be avoided during pregnancy and by those who suffer from epilepsy, and should not be used by anyone on a course of homeopathic treatment. Test for allergies by applying the rosemary oil to the inside of your wrist 24 hours before doing this exercise.

WHAT TO DO

1 Rub a little rosemary oil into your candle and light it to mark the start of the actions to come. The scent of the rosemary should help bring what you have learned from the previous lunar phase into action here. Make sure you are sitting comfortably, preferably with a view of the crescent moon in the sky. Think about the kinds of things you would like to achieve in this waxing phase.

2 When you feel ready, pick up the first piece of clay and roll it into a ball between your palms.

3 Then pick up another piece and mould it into the first piece so that it becomes a larger ball, soft between your palms. Say to yourself, 'As the moon grows, so ... (name one of your goals or projects) is growing, better and better. Growing, growing, growing, better, better, better.' Repeat this to yourself as often as you like as you pick up piece after piece of clay to add to your ball. As you do this, imagine the success of your goal or project growing with it if you can.

4 When you feel your clay ball is large enough, push your finger down through the middle to create a hole and insert the ribbon through it. Tie a knot at the end so it won't slip out, leave a loop at the top to enable you to hang it up and push the clay

around the end of the ribbon, so it won't come loose.

5 Now push coloured pins into the clay, one by one, naming each after a positive factor relating to your new goal or project, according to colour. For example, you might choose green to symbolize financial success, red for heightened energy and blue for clarity. Just use whatever colour associations feel right to you.

6 When you have finished, put a few drops of rosemary oil onto the base of the ribbon and hang your 'Success Ball' by your desk or somewhere else that will allow you to see it when you need motivation.

7 Then dab a drop of the diluted rosemary oil between your eyes to help with remembrance, saying, 'I see clearly what I want in life', avoiding contact with eyes. Next, do the same on your chest, saying, 'I am full of courage and enterprise', and on your palms, saying, 'My hands work for me to create wonderful things'.

8 Also anoint any other part of your body that is involved in your project, such as your feet if lots of walking is involved or your ears if it is music and so on. Avoid contact with the mouth, however, as essential oils should never be ingested. Let the moon bring you success.

FULL MOON

Full moon is a time when the lunar powers are, in some way, at their maximum. We may feel more in tune with our instincts, and our emotions may be stronger during this phase. It can be a magical time, when the spirit world seems close; a time of fruition and balance or, in keeping with the capricious nature of the moon, it can be a time when things get a little out of control. Full moon offers inspiration and an opportunity to celebrate life and accept all our feelings, thus feeling complete.

Think about the fulfilment and satisfaction in your life – especially about all the things you have achieved in life, from being in a happy relationship, raising a family, building a successful career and having great friends to much smaller things, like a perfectly baked cake, a well-organized closet space or a beautifully maintained garden. Write these things in your lunar journal – you will probably think of new things every full moon. It is a good idea to celebrate the full moon with friends – compliment each other on your achievements and raise a glass to success.

It is especially advised to celebrate love and relationships during full moon, so buy or pick a few fresh leaves of lemon balm (*Melissa officinalis*), which is ruled by the moon, and soak them for an hour or so in grape juice. Leave them to infuse in the light of the moon, if you can, and then share a cup of the resulting mixture with your loved one as a sign that your love is true and lasting.

To boost your attractiveness, why not have a full-moon beauty bath? Light six deep pink candles in your bathroom, add a few drops of vanilla oil (see caution, opposite) to the water and sprinkle the surface liberally with rose petals. These may be fresh or dried, but so much the better if you picked them yourself at full moon! Lie in your bath, thinking about every compliment you have ever received and imagine you are absorbing beauty from the water and rose petals. When you are ready, dry yourself and rub in some scented body lotion.

THE MOTHER GODDESS

The full moon is often linked to the Mother Goddess (see page 53), and Isis, from ancient Egypt, provides a particularly powerful association. She ruled Egypt alongside her husband Osiris, until he was murdered by his brother Set, who took away and dismembered his body. Isis showed her strength and resolve by managing to find 12 of the 13 body pieces, reassemble them, add a gold penis in place of his missing one and conceive Horus, the sun God. Osiris then took on the role of King of the Dead, while Isis continued to rule the living with wisdom and benevolence. She is a role model for power and strength. Some people believe that the 13 pieces of the body relate to the 13 rounds of the zodiac that the moon makes in a year, one of which has become 'lost' in a 12-month calendar.

A TIME OF FULFILMENT

During full moon, it is best to adorn your moon altar with objects that represent fulfilment, blessing, passion and enchantment. Candles may be white (appropriate for the full moon), silver (a lunar metal and

therefore colour) or blood-red (for full moon is a 'full-blooded' time). Flowers to pick include lilies, irises, lotus or red roses, and crystals might include rubies, garnets and carnelian, or moonstone, beryl, sapphire and chalcedony. Cards or pictures that remind you of strong feelings may also be beneficial, as can figures or images of dogs, wolves and hares – the animals traditionally associated with full moon.

VANILLA OIL CAUTION

Vanilla oil has sensual, seductive associations but, as is the case when using any essential oils, it is best to do an allergy test of it on a small patch of skin before adding it to your bath, as recommended in the exercise steps. And remember, never use essential oils internally.

FULL MOON EXERCISE
FOR INSPIRATION

Full moon gives you access to the powers of the natural world at their height, and offers you an opportunity to get in touch with your own deepest wellsprings of inspiration and intuition. It may also reveal to you your emotions, and while this can be hard at times, recognizing and accepting them brings strength. You will enjoy the celebratory exercise below most if you are outside, when the full moon is in the sky. If this isn't possible, settle yourself comfortably by an open window. It is especially enjoyable if you perform it with a close friend or lover.

WHAT YOU WILL NEED

- an oil burner
- matches
- ylang ylang oil (see below)
- a large candle
- matches
- two bowls (preferably silver, white or earthenware; avoid anything synthetic)
- water
- a white towel
- an attractive glass with a stem
- some beautifully fragranced white and red flowers
- some delicious white and red coloured food and drinks, (such as grapes, white cheese, melon, yogurt, white chocolate, strawberries, red apples and cranberry juice. Organic foods are best and meat should be avoided)

YLANG YLANG OIL CAUTION

Ylang ylang oil is a soothing, calming oil, which aids self-expression. However, it is advised that you only use it in small amounts for short periods of time, as you may find the perfume can become too heavy after a while and potentially even cause nausea or headaches. Please note that the use of ylang ylang oil is not recommended for people with low blood pressure. It is always best to do a small patch test on your skin before using an essential oil in any substantial measure.

WHAT TO DO

1 Place an array of white and red flowers around the place you choose to do this exercise to act as a devotional background. Then place some ylang ylang oil in your oil burner and heat it. The fragrance will help to encourage the flow of emotions, so let your feelings come to the surface, whatever they may be.

2 Fill your two bowls with water, take one of them and see if you can catch the reflection of the full moon in it. If the sky is clouded or you cannot see the moon, you can substitute the moon with a large lit candle. After a few moments, wash your face and hands in the water, saying, 'My emotions flow freely and good things are growing for me'. Repeat this a few times. Then set the water to one side, to be poured out onto the earth later, and dry yourself on the towel.

3 Now take the second bowl and again try to catch the moon or candle's reflection in the surface of the water. Say, 'The bright moon is a symbol of inspiration. I shall see deeply and my instincts will run true.' Scoop up a little of the water in your glass and sip it, imagining bright ideas flowing into your body. Now wash your face, hands and any other part of your body that you feel is appropriate while affirming your

wish for intuition and inspiration. Use the towel again to dry yourself.

4 Take up the ylang ylang oil, diluted in a carrier oil such as grapeseed (one drop of ylang ylang oil to one teaspoon of carrier oil). Place a little of the oil on each wrist, saying, 'With this I affirm that my body is in rhythm with nature'. Place some of the oil near your navel, saying, 'With this I affirm that I nurture all that is productive in my life', and place some of the oil on your forehead, between your eyes, saying, 'With this I affirm that I see all that is inspiring.'

5 Complete the exercise by eating the white and red foods, reminding yourself about all the good things in life. Try to catch the moon's reflection in the glass as you drink if possible. Remember that you are affirming to your subconscious mind that the world is full of beauty, which will give you inspiration throughout life.

WANING MOON

When the moon is waning we are in a period of decrease, withdrawal and turning inwards. The perfect sphere of the full moon gradually wears away, appearing later and later during the night until only the wan crescent loiters in the dawn. This is the best time for anything involving banishing, undoing and expelling.

The waning moon has often been thought of as a negative phase but it can be both peaceful and productive. Because the waning moon can have an eerie feel, it is also thought to be a time to see spirits. Old country lore states that to encourage the sight of spirits you should burn an incense of willow bark (willow is sacred to the moon) mixed with sandalwood. To rid yourself of any desire that you feel has become destructive – especially a sexual one – eat cucumber as the moon is waning, imagining those unwanted feelings dampened and shrivelling. If possible, do this while you can see the waning crescent in the sky, and ask the moon to take your unhealthy desires away from you, into oblivion.

GODDESS OF WISDOM

The waning moon is associated with the Crone, goddess of old age and wisdom (see page 53). The Greek goddess Hecate is one of the most well-known examples. She was believed to stalk the highways and byways on moonless nights, lighting her way with a flaming torch, her savage dogs at her heels. Sorcerers studied her ways behind locked doors and left offerings for her at any place where the road forked three ways. Indeed, many believed that she could look in three directions at once, having three heads; that of a dog, a snake and a horse. She ruled the spirits of the night and the souls of the dead, and sacrifices of black lambs, dogs and honey were made to her in order that she might keep the dark forces, over which she was believed to preside, at bay. Hecate may appear sinister, but she shows us that by facing our fears, we can transform them – and ourselves – and become more powerful. If there is something in life that really scares you, such as public speaking, making a commitment in a relationship, enclosed spaces or spiders, the waning moon is the best time to take steps to eradicate these fears. Behavioural therapy, cognitive therapy and hypnotherapy are all recommended. The 'triple' theme in the story of Hecate can be seen as relating to mind, body and spirit: mentally, you may decide to be free of old habits and patterns; physically, you may wish to detoxify your body, weed your garden or get rid of rubbish; and spiritually, you may decide to purge unwanted emotions from the past.

It is best to place objects on your moon altar that remind you of tranquillity and detachment. You might choose candles in harmonious colours such as violet, blue or deep green to encourage meditation, peace and inwardness. Flowers might be forget-me-nots, heather, lilac, or you could arrange apples in a purple bowl with fresh herbs such as lemon balm and rosemary (for remembrance). Crystals to choose from include amethyst, aquamarine, alexandrite or labradorite, and pictures or

ornaments of animals such as serpents, spiders, moths, bats and black cats would be good, as these creatures represent the darker, more mysterious element of the moon. Pictures that evoke images of farewell are also suitable, such as sunsets or sleeping figures.

WANING MOON EXERCISE TO
BE FREE OF NEGATIVE EMOTIONS

At times we all experience negative emotions such as anger, jealousy, envy and even hatred. There is nothing wrong with such feelings; it is important that they are expressed and dealt with, rather than being repressed, as we have a right to them and they are telling us something valid. However, there are times when it is simply unproductive – and possibly even harmful to ourselves – to let a feeling linger. An example might be anger at a lover who has long since departed from our life or envy of a friend even when that friend is truly kind, and when we ourselves also have many things of which to be proud. When you need to let go and move on, the waning moon can be a great help. The exercise below is simple but you are advised to take it slowly and spend as much time as you need in introspection.

WHAT YOU WILL NEED

- a violet or purple candle
- matches
- a stone
- some chalk
- a paper bag
- some oil of myrrh or cypress
- an oil-burner
- an old black scarf or piece of fabric (that you are happy to discard)

A NOTE ON THIS EXERCISE

This exercise involves being outdoors, which may require some forward planning, but will enable you to draw on the healing powers of nature. You will need to be within walking distance of a stream, pool or lake as it will give the rite more power. Wait until you are sure the moon has passed into the waning phase, at least four days after full moon.

WHAT TO DO

1 Take a walk in the moonless dusk, in the country or in parkland, and look for a black or grey stone that is large enough to write a few letters on. As you do this, think about the feelings that you want to be rid of and strengthen your resolution to be free from them.

2 Heat the myrrh or cypress oil in the oil-burner so that its sombre fragrance rises. Light the candle and sit with the black scarf around your shoulders. Think about the feeling that you wish to expel. Make it into a creature or object if you wish and imagine it shrinking, entering the stone. If you cannot visualize this, don't worry – just tell yourself it is happening or imagine the stone getting heavier.

3 When you are ready, use the white chalk to write a word or a few word initials that represent how you feel.

4 Blow out your candle and, with the scarf still around your shoulders, walk towards the lake or river, taking your stone and paper bag with you.

5 When you get there, stand for a moment saying something like, 'I strongly affirm that I am cleansing myself of my sorrow/ anger/fear/jealousy. They are going into the darkness, out of my life. I shall now be free'. Throw the stone with all your might into the water and pull off the black scarf, stuffing it into the paper bag to be burned later.

6 Congratulate yourself and take it easy for the next week or so, pampering yourself and resting, if you wish. When the silver sickle appears again in the evening sky it will be time for new plans.

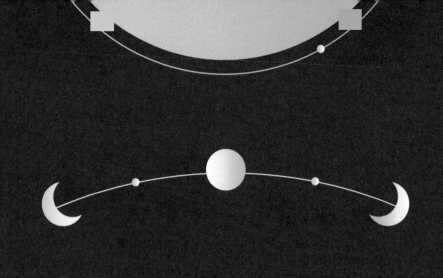

MOON PHASE
LIFE PLANNING

The following pages will help you to get the most out of your life and to put your energies where they will be most effectual, in tune with the lunar phases and your moon sign. The information is arranged, for your ease of use, in four sections: Health and Beauty, Love and Relationships, Home and Garden and Career and Finances. Advice is given on what you might find it best to do and to avoid during each of the four lunar phases. There are certain aspects of life that may not fall strictly within the four categories. However, it will be possible to glean the information you need with a bit of sensible tweaking. Each lifestyle section then ends with a sign-by-sign synopsis for that area of your life. You can use this information to find out what type of things it is best for you to plan or do during the current moon sign, which you can work out using the charts on pages 132–141. Firstly, work out the current moon sign and then read whichever entry is relevant to that.

Naturally, it won't always be possible to choose the timing of things in life but there is no need to worry about this. If you become attuned to the waxing and waning feelings, you will soon have an instinct for what is right during each phase, and can adjust accordingly.

DARK MOON—NEW MOON

This phase of the moon is about making plans and letting go of old, bad habits, so let yourself feel excited by the possibilities. Are you satisfied with your diet, lifestyle and appearance? Now is the time to think about this and to consider changes. Take a long, hard look at yourself, and be honest, but also realistic. What are you really not happy with? What might be achieved? How much time do you have to devote to exercise and beauty care? All these are things to ponder.

Entertain any new idea about change in your appearance, however far-fetched it may seem at first. You will find that there are many ways to make yourself feel better if you keep an open mind. Would you like a change of image, or to try new styles or colours of clothes?

Sit quietly and get in touch with your body. What sort of exercise would feel best, and which parts of your body feel the need for most movement and stimulation? If something slightly unusual comes to mind, don't dismiss it. Instead, try to explore why you feel what you feel. Are you putting up with a troublesome condition like eczema or migraines? Maybe you could try

new approaches to alleviate the problem. If you need more exercise, plan how you are going to fit it into your schedule.

Be honest with yourself about what you are eating. Do you ever eat for comfort or out of boredom? Are you consuming too many processed foods, eating what and when it suits other people rather than yourself, or in any other way putting into your body what it does not want? Remember, you are what you eat, so consider how can you change your eating habits for the better.

THINGS TO DO

- Start a health and beauty notebook and write in it all the things that you would like to achieve or that you think might make you feel good about yourself.

- Find out about the latest creams and lotions, and what they could do for your skin. Make a note of anything that particularly appeals to you.

- Talk to a beautician or hairdresser about making changes in your appearance, if you want this. Listen to what they say even if it does not fit your initial idea of how you should look. Are you limiting yourself? Might it be an idea to expand your perspectives?

- Have investigative health and beauty treatments, such as skin-typing or BMI (body mass index) measurement – this is a time for finding out all you can about yourself.

- Gather information from health clubs and gyms in your area. Visit several if you like and sample what they have to offer, without committing. Make sure that what you are considering will realistically fit around your other commitments.

- If you have a troublesome health condition that needs treatment, consider alternative therapies, such as reiki, shiatsu massage or reflexology. Research these on the Internet or in your local library. Talk to friends who have had treatments and talk to therapists themselves.

- If you need to lose weight, think carefully about how to go about it.

- If you need to eat more healthily, look through recipe books, create sensible shopping lists and make sure you are well-informed about nutrition. You might like to see a nutritional consultant to test for any food intolerances or just for some general guidance.

THINGS TO AVOID

- Don't make any major changes in your appearance straight away. This is a time for reflecting and gathering ideas. You need to wait a few days before you can feel sure what is right for you.

- Don't spend a lot on cosmetics – you might change your mind before full moon.

- It is best not to be too impulsive about exercise routines. Don't pay your subscription at a new gym until you have thought it through and tried out the equipment.

- Don't commit to doing exercise with friends unless you are sure you have the time and energy for it. It is too soon in the lunar month to join a new sports team unless you have already been thinking about it for several weeks.

- Don't rush to a new therapist and demand a special type of massage or other treatment just because you like the sound of it, or because it has worked for a friend. Find out more first.

- However great a new diet sounds, resist the impulse to buy loads of different foods, or empty your kitchen cabinets of the old ones. Give yourself another few days to be quite sure that any new eating plan is right for you.

- Don't just reach for any new herbal treatment or medicine that makes wonderful promises. It is probably too soon to be sure what is truly going to suit your body.

- Try not to let yourself feel too down or negative about your appearance and health. This time is best spent thinking – as a prelude to the change and improvement that you can start to bring about during the moon's waxing phase.

HEALTH AND BEAUTY
WAXING MOON

Now is the time to make choices from the ideas you considered at dark–new moon and put them into practice. You will probably have plenty of energy and enthusiasm, so make sure you use this wisely. Give yourself time to get into your stride. If you have decided that no changes are necessary, then simply take up your normal activities with renewed vigour.

If you want to make any particular changes in your appearance, now is the perfect time to do it, so make that appointment with the hairdresser or with the beautician as soon as you can. You will probably feel more positive about life if you try out something different, however small a thing it may seem. And if you are at the point in your life where a completely new image seems the right thing to do, then this phase of the moon will usher it in with a swing.

This is a good time to start trying to lose weight, if necessary, but the weight may not fall away as quickly as you like, because your body is likely to absorb and retain fluids. It would be a mistake, however, to reduce fluid intake because things will level out as

the month progresses. Use the enthusiasm of this phase to put the things you want in motion without too many expectations.

Your skin will probably absorb creams more effectively during this phase, so start any beauty treatment that depends on this, as it will, in all probability, show results more quickly than at other times. It takes about two weeks for new habits to become established in the subconscious, so you will have more than enough time for your new routine to become engrained before the next new moon.

THINGS TO DO

- Embark on a nutritious diet and start taking well-chosen food supplements if necessary. If you need to build muscle, put on weight or boost your vitamin and mineral intake, the waxing moon will give you the most benefit, most quickly.

- Stock up on and start eating plenty of fresh, healthy foods – such as fruit, vegetables, nuts and seeds – about three days after new moon, as it will be easier than usual to be enthusiastic and positive about weight-loss diet during this phase.

- Buy yourself an outfit in a completely different style or colour than usual. Bright colours may be especially appealing and more modern, daring or alternative clothes could feel right for you now.

- Arrange any beauty therapy that mildly stimulates the skin, encouraging the growth of new skin cells. If your skin is dry it will absorb creams better now. However, greasy skin may become more oily, so try to use gentle cleansers more frequently.

- If you are thinking about a different hairstyle, go for it! Changing your cut or colour will seem most exciting now, but only if you have carefully considered at dark moon what will best suit you.

- Start doing regular sport or exercise. Even if it is winter, evening activities are likely to seem more appealing during this lunar phase.

- A well-chosen alternative therapy will do you considerable good so make your appointment for acupuncture, massage, homoeopathy or whatever you have decided to embark on, as soon as possible after new moon.

THINGS TO AVOID

- Don't grab at something new just because it is new. Take action based on the decisions you made as to what is right for you during the dark–new moon phase.

- There's no need to worry if things don't go smoothly at first. You are only starting out, so remember to be patient.

- It is advised not to opt for an expensive new look that is too different from your usual image unless you are either extremely sure that it is what you want or it is something that you can readily change back from, such as a wig or a hired garment.

- There's no point in dieting too ferociously – you may get fed up and give up, or, worse, you could harm your health. Why not concentrate on developing good eating habits instead?

- If you are exercising, be very careful not to overdo things. This is especially important if you are trying out new exercises. Take things slowly at first because you may be more prone to pulling a muscle or hurting yourself during this lunar phase.

- If you have joined a sports team, try not to be too competitive. The point is to be fit, healthy and to have fun – and not necessarily to win all of the time.

- On a similar note, don't be too determined to beat your personal best when exercising. It is your fitness that matters, not how good, fast or strong you are.

- Don't go to extremes with your skin. Blemishes tend to appear more readily with a waxing moon, but they should be treated gently. Don't use too many astringents on oily skin and don't smother dry skin in rich creams – use everything in moderation.

HEALTH AND BEAUTY
FULL MOON

The full moon is a time for celebration, enjoyment and a little bit of excess. Your energies will probably be at their peak and you may be able to make do with less sleep. However, you may also feel that everything becomes too much and feel suddenly over-committed. If this happens, be prepared to just sit back and relax a little.

The climax of full moon sometimes reveals things that are not working, and if any of your projects seem unsatisfactory, do not be afraid to abandon them. Your feelings will make themselves heard, loud and clear. Even when things are going really well, full moon can bring some surprises. For instance, your weight may have been dropping on your diet, only for you to find that at full moon it has gone up, or stayed the same. Things can easily go a little crazy at full moon, but this will stabilize in a few days time.

You may feel the need for a treat of some kind at the moment and if so, by all means indulge yourself. It is better to do this than to attempt to repress your desires, for they are then likely to overtake you in some extreme way that you might regret. Cravings can be at their maximum, and moderation is especially

hard to achieve during this phase. Remember, this does not mean that there is anything wrong with you or that you are weak-willed – you are simply tuned in to the lunar 'vibe'. Find ways of enjoying it, if you can. The more beneficial treats you can give your body, the more you are likely to be content and able to steer clear of anything unhealthy.

THINGS TO DO

- You can achieve a great deal in terms of your appearance and well-being at full moon, but you need to be a little self-indulgent as well!

- If you would like something delicious, such as chocolate, ice-cream, cake, or your favourite tipple, then try to build this into your diet, or allow yourself a little lapse. Beware, however, that the time of the full moon is the time you're most likely to overdo things.

- Have a beauty therapy that is a real indulgence, such as a facial, massage, manicure or pedicure. The full moon is a time for glamour.

- Treat yourself to a wonderful new garment in a luxurious fabric or a dramatic colour or style.

- Buy yourself some fantastic new jewellery, especially in silver, as this is a metal with strong lunar associations.

- Go on a shopping spree for new clothes, fragrances, beauty products, health foods or sports gear.

- If you feel very energetic, do use this in your exercise routine, or you could become very frustrated. Go on just that little bit longer at the gym, play an extra round of tennis or golf or walk for a bit longer.

- Schedule that big friendly match at this time – it will probably be more fun.

- However, do be extra-careful. The full moon can be a time of more accidents and increased chance of bleeding, so ensure that you have the first-aid kit nearby!

- If you have found a particular therapy to be very beneficial, and your therapist to be trustworthy, make an appointment for a special treatment session at full moon.

THINGS TO AVOID

- If you have a lapse, don't go overboard, saying to yourself 'Oh well, that's it! I've broken my diet, so I may as well binge!' So many diets fail on that all-or-nothing approach, and it's easiest to fall for it at full moon. Remember, every day is a new day.

- By the same token, don't go crazy in the other direction, by starving yourself or going on a crash diet. It won't work long-term. In fact, it is likely to have the opposite effect.

- Don't splash out on a whole new wardrobe, some expensive new exercise machine or anything costly or extreme where you cannot get your money back if you decide not to keep it. You may not be thinking clearly at the moment.

- Don't take too many food supplements or herbal remedies, as excess of any sort can be more harmful now.

- Try not to push yourself too hard. Pressure may seem great at this time and you may feel caught up in things that are out of your control, but you need to pull back if you feel over-wrought.

- Don't involve yourself in any particularly demanding and competitive sports. You may have fantastic energy, but you are also more likely to lose your temper or have an accident.

- If you are having any therapy that places demands on you, such as some form of counselling or massage, consider avoiding this around the time of the full moon, as it may prove too much for you.

HEALTH AND BEAUTY
WANING MOON

This phase of the moon is the best time to banish all those beauty problems from your life – for good. The lunar influence is about cutting down, receding and fading, and this can be translated to countless things, from body fat to skin blemishes. However, if some of the things that you have been trying to do have not been right for you, it will now become obvious to you that there is no point in continuing them, so shed anything from your routine that is not beneficial to you and save your energy for something more worthwhile.

Your exercise routine does not have to lose its momentum. Think of it as being your way of expelling lack of physical fitness from your life. It may feel during this phase as if the pace is slower and there are fewer demands on your time. Although you should always be careful, you are less likely to overdo things or to pull a muscle when the moon is on the wane.

Substances are less readily absorbed by the body during the moon's waning phase, which makes it a good time for trying to lose weight: what you may lack in energy and determination may be more than made up for by the lunar climate, as fluid retention is less likely to be a problem.

It may be more possible to unwind and relax at the end of the day, as the pace slows down. Take advantage of this to de-stress, gradually turning more and more inwards as the moon comes closer to the dark moon period.

THINGS TO DO

- Lunar energies are diminishing now, but that doesn't mean there aren't many things you can achieve at the moment. In fact, it may seem as though your choices are clearer and simpler at this less hectic time.

- This is a wonderful time to go on a detox diet. Your body will more readily expel toxins, leaving you feeling cleansed. You can detox by cutting out alcohol, caffeine, dairy, meat and wheat from your diet, or by going organic, or by following your chosen method from a book. Herbal detox preparations are available and the simple grapefruit, either eaten or used as essential oil, is effective.

- Try to get as many early nights as you can, benefiting from the increasing rest to re-charge your system.

- Consider a deep-cleansing facial or body wrap with your beautician.

- Maintain your enthusiasm for your diet. You may find you are losing weight more easily, which will be a boost.

- Take special care that your facial cleanser is effective – use face packs, scrubs and toners with extra enthusiasm!

- Tackle any blockage problems such as constipation or congestion with a mild herbal remedy, such as liquorice or eucalyptus.

- Concentrate on endurance sports as you are less likely to overdo things or 'burn out' during this phase of the moon.

- Go through your closets and review their contents. Do you have any garments that you no longer like or need? Perhaps some no longer fit you, or suit your lifestyle. You will find them easier to get rid of now, so be ruthless – bag them up and send them to charity.

THINGS TO AVOID

- Don't waste your precious time and energy on anything fruitless. If something is turning out not to be worthwhile, abandon it. Soon dark moon will be here and you can make new plans.

- Do not, however, give up when you've only just started. For instance, just because your stomach muscles seem no firmer just yet, that is no reason to abandon a good exercise routine. You will just have to give it more time.

- It's best not to have any major change of image or style right now. If a situation or event calls for something new, for example a new job or a wedding, then make only moderate and flexible changes, such as with accessories, a pair of shoes or a single garment.

- Don't opt for a totally new hairstyle or dramatic change of hair colour. It's fine to have a routine haircut or a touch-up of your roots, however, if you so desire.

- Don't try totally new recipes. If you have to be inventive for a dinner party, or for your own diet, then make changes with salads, side dishes and dressings rather than trying a major new dish.

- This isn't a good time to start a new diet or a fresh exercise routine. You are likely to run out of steam quickly or simply change your mind at dark moon.

- Don't spend a lot on beauty products, and don't experiment. Just re-stock with your regular products and wait for new moon to think up new things.

- Try not to allow yourself to fall into negative thinking patterns. Focus instead on your good points and count what you have achieved in your life, even if it is not quite as much as you would have liked.

HEALTH AND BEAUTY
THROUGH THE MOON SIGNS

ARIES

Concentrate on your hairstyle, hair colour and any health matters to do with your head. If you suffer from migraines, or similar, research and take new remedies for your ailment. An Aries moon is a good time to buy a new hat or earrings, as Aries rules the head. While the moon is in Aries, stress is more likely than usual to cause headaches, so make a special effort to relax. Indian head massage will be especially beneficial and enjoyable, as will facials. You may feel especially competitive in your exercise routine and can achieve much, but do not take risks or strain yourself.

TAURUS

Buy beautiful jewellery of all kinds, but especially necklaces, as Taurus rules the neck. Choose a necklace to team with each of your outfits, to complete your look. This is also a good time to buy scarves, either as decorative accessories or for warmth – or both! Pay particular attention to the skin on your neck, cleansing and using a deep moisturizer to keep this stretched area supple and graceful. Invest in a luscious, earthy fragrance, for use especially on the pulse points beneath your ears. Exercises to get rid of a double chin, or to extend the mobility of the neck are best embarked upon now, especially if the moon is waxing.

GEMINI

You are likely to want to make changes to your appearance with a Gemini moon, especially if it is waxing. You may feel restless. Exercise in short bursts to alleviate boredom, or if you work out in a gym, make sure there is something interesting on the over-head TV! Your diet will be easiest to follow if you have lots of different foodstuffs. Bracelets and gloves are a good buy, as Gemini rules the arms and hands. Book yourself in for a manicure and choose some bright nail-polish. Shoulder massage will be especially relaxing

and decongestants for the lungs
will have good effect.

CANCER

If you have a tendency to comfort-
eat, this may be stimulated by
the moon in Cancer. Find ways of
making yourself feel nurtured that
are not going to be detrimental
to your chosen eating plan. Look
after your stomach, taking herbal
remedies such as fennel if you have
indigestion. Swimming and water-
sports are good exercises now.
Shirts and blouses can be shopped
for, as Cancer rules the breasts
and stomach. Choose smooth, soft
fabrics in pastel colours, or buy
something nostalgic or retro that
makes you feel romantic when you
wear it. Look also for delicate items
of silver jewellery.

LEO

Dramatic Leo moon puts you in
the mood for glamour. Shop for
gold jewellery or designer labels.
Leo moon focuses on the heart,
so check your heart rate when
exercising to keep track of your
metabolic rate. If you do not
already do so, plan to exercise

each day to a point where your
heart rate rises to make you slightly
out of breath for ten minutes.
Focus on aspects of your diet that
promote a healthy heart, such
as Omega 3 and Omega 6 oils,
which can be found in foods such
as nuts, seeds and certain fish.
You are likely to want the best of
everything, so invest in organic
foods that nourish the body and up
the feel-good factor.

VIRGO

You will want to think especially
about your health under a Virgo
moon and will probably feel like
shopping for order and hygiene
– buying hairbrushes, toothpaste,
clothes hangers and other such
practical items, all of the best
quality you can afford. You will
also feel more in tune with the lunar
vibe if your appearance is neat
and tidy. Pay special attention to
your stomach as Virgo rules the
intestines and take gentle herbal
remedies such as liquorice if you
are sluggish. Plan to eat more
fibre if necessary. You may be
rather self-critical in terms of your
exercise, so remind yourself that
you do not have to achieve
great things and be positive
about yourself.

LIBRA

Ease up on exercise at this time if you want to. You may find you prefer exercising with friends, or dancing in couples to more strenuous sports. Sweet foods may appeal, so treat yourself to some exotic fruits. Remind yourself that any diet has lapses, and if you experience this, it is simply normal. If you have to buy clothes for a special occasion, now is the time. Libra moon helps you co-ordinate and balance your body shape with the correct styles.

SCORPIO

You may feel like a total change of image, whatever the lunar phase. Any extreme changes you make should be carefully considered – this is a good time for them, but only if they are right for you. Dramatic colours such as black and deep reds may appeal, and you are likely to want to dress to attract potential partners. You may feel more passionate than usual about exercise, but do not punish your body. Instead go for long walks in the country, to allow you to think. A radical new approach to your diet may appeal to you under a

Scorpio moon. Purging treatments such as colonic hydrotherapy are in tune with this.

SAGITTARIUS

This is an energetic time so it is good to push yourself, but remember your limitations. Your mind may be occupied with lofty thoughts, so any eating regime could prove too much. Remind yourself that your body is your temple. Laughter is a great boost to the immune system. Sagittarius stimulates the sense of humour, so take advantage of this by spending time with entertaining friends. Any problems with hips and thighs should respond well to appropriate treatment under a Sagittarius moon. Shop for trendy sports gear, for you will want to create the best impression possible. Fresh air is especially necessary and beneficial at this time.

CAPRICORN

Shop for formal, elegant clothes, such as business suits, and designer watches as you want to dress to impress under a Capricorn moon. Pay special attention to your skin, nourishing it and investing in any top-quality treatment that has been thoroughly tried and tested. Be careful that you do not take things too seriously. If you are involved in sport, don't forget that it is supposed to be fun! Skeletal problems, especially of the lower legs and knees, respond well to some loving care right now, so make an appointment with your chiropractor, osteopath or masseur if you have problems in this area. Most important of all, do not repress your feelings.

AQUARIUS

This is a good time to explore totally new ways of doing things, including eating healthily, joining a new hi-tech gym or maybe detoxing your body, but do not do it just for the sake of it. At the very least, get yourself a pedometer to monitor how far you walk in a day. Fresh air will be especially inviting.

You may have an urge to buy socks and shoes at this time, as Aquarius rules the ankles. Try out the latest electronic beauty treatments or healing therapies based on subtle energies, such as acupuncture or reiki. Any problems with your ankles in particular should respond best now.

PISCES

You are unlikely to feel very energetic with Pisces moon. However, water sports such as swimming, sailing and surfing may inspire you due to their association with water, Pisces being a water sign. It may be very hard to limit intake of food, drugs and alcohol. Don't seek to soothe emotions through these. Instead, find a sympathetic shoulder to cry on. Pay special attention to your feet, having a luxurious pedicure, nourishing your feet with a lotion containing essential oil of peppermint or lemon, and choosing a wonderful coloured polish for your toenails if you wish. A foot-based therapy such as reflexology will be especially beneficial at this time. Shop also for footwear of all descriptions.

LOVE AND RELATIONSHIPS
DARK MOON—NEW MOON

This is a time for deep reflection and introspection, which provides a good opportunity for you to stand back from any relationships in your life and take a long, hard look at how they are going. It is all too easy to get into a rut or to accept things that are less than satisfactory simply because they have become a habit. Dark moon is a good time to become aware of any unhealthy emotional patterns you have fallen into.

If you are in a committed relationship, and wish to stay committed, how might you improve matters? Do you need to spend more quality time with your partner, to talk more openly with each other or to be more impulsive and romantic? Remember that admitting to yourself that something is not satisfactory in a relationship in no way means that you have to end it. You could simply try to make changes, if you like, or you may decide that you can live with the things that aren't quite right in order to benefit from the positive elements. For instance, you may realize you are happy to accept that your relationship lacks a little excitement if it gives you the support and comfort you need. Becoming aware of this willingness to accept your relationship as 'good enough' may foster a sense of contentment, as opposed to a constant sense of ill-defined dissatisfaction.

If you don't have a partner, but would like one, now is the time to think up strategies for meeting new people. Similarly, if your social circle is too narrow, think about ways you might expand it. Relationships with friends are just as important as a one-to-one relationship with a partner, so review your interaction with friends, too. However, it is best not to put your ideas into practice until the moon waxes.

THINGS TO DO

- Create time alone to think about the relationships in your life. What is good about them? And what is not so good? How would you like to change this? Write your thoughts down in your lunar journal.

- Talk openly and peaceably with your partner about your relationship, how you can make it better and what each would like the other to do. Be positive and clear, and concentrate on how you feel within yourself, rather than blaming the other person. Resist the temptation to dwell on past mistakes, but if something really is eating away at you, it may be best to bring it out into the open.

- Spend time alone with anyone that you are really close to, doing all the things that you love to do together, without interruption, and talking about your plans for the future.

- If a love affair has already ended and you are trying to move on, now may be a good time to burn old love letters.

- If you are single, gather information on dating agencies, singles clubs and other ways to meet prospective partners.

- Decide, realistically, what you would like in a partner and affirm to yourself that you are going to get it.

- If you want to make new friends, give some thought to how you could meet them. Be sensible and true to yourself: there is no point in hoping to meet kindred spirits in your local pub if you are a teetotal opera fan!

- Ask someone you trust and respect for their honest opinion about something personal, face the truth about their answer and make plans for changes in light of it as the moon waxes.

THINGS TO AVOID

- Beware of falling into an overly negative mood. Elements of your relationships that are not so good may look even worse now, so take a balanced outlook.

- Don't fall prey to suspicions – if you have doubts, ask.

- Don't dwell on past mistakes – they are in the past. Learn from them, and they will have had a purpose. Then move on.

- Don't firmly commit yourself to anything until waxing moon is established. For example, this may not be the best time to get engaged or to decide to move in together. Getting the keys for a new home would, however, be a separate issue as you would have made the decision to live together long ago and, in any case, is something you might not be able to control in terms of timing.

- Don't go overboard on a new relationship. If it seems good, nurture it carefully, but keep it low-key for a while.

- Don't expect your sex drive to be at its highest during dark moon as you are likely to feel that deeper things are more important, such as where you are going in life.

- Don't pay subscriptions to clubs, dating agencies and magazines until the new moon has started to appear.

- This is not the best time to throw a big party to gather friends together, as everyone may be a bit subdued. Small gatherings of intimate friends are better during this phase.

- Try not to take the things that people say too much to heart – you may be hearing only the negative parts.

- Don't put all your efforts into seducing an attractive stranger. It might work out, but it is less likely to during this phase.

LOVE AND RELATIONSHIPS
WAXING MOON

Use the waxing moon phase to expand and develop relationships of all sorts, and to work through the issues related to them. During the dark–new period you will have thought things through, formed ideas and made plans in your head. Now is the time to start putting them into practice.

It is beneficial at this time to keep a sense of adventure and be prepared to experiment. What have you got to lose? Creating and seizing opportunities gives you the chance of finding a wonderful new relationship. You may have to kiss a lot of frogs before you find your prince, but it is useful to remember that everything that does not work out can teach you something and bring you closer to your goal.

If you are already in a committed relationship, you can explore new ideas and places together, and try to surprise each other more. The waxing moon can put some extra spice back into your love life. If you are dating, but not yet fully committed, the waxing moon may encourage you to get closer.

The same approaches apply to friendships. If you would like to make new friends, then get out and meet new people, anywhere and any way you can. Accept any invitation, however bizarre it may seem, for it may turn out to be productive and entertaining. If you are a naturally reserved person, the waxing moon will give you some encouragement and confidence. Be yourself but also try to tune into the lunar flow and therefore not restrict yourself too much during this phase.

THINGS TO DO

- If you are single, now is the time to get out as much as possible to anywhere you might meet possible partners. You may wish to try online dating.

- If you feel attracted to someone, be brave and ask them out on a date.

- If you are in a relationship, leave notes for your lover in unexpected places, telling him or her what you would like to do when you are alone. It is also a good time to write love letters and provocative texts to prospective partners.

- Waxing moon is a time for spontaneity. You don't have to do the same things every evening. What do you really feel like doing together on the spur of the moment?

- Go and see romantic and exciting films or plays. These will give your imagination a boost.

- Place your confidence in lovers and friends by taking small risks with them, such as speaking more openly in their company or going to entirely new places together.

- Do active, productive things with your friends, like shopping, planning an event or party, doing the garden together or whatever else appeals.

- Get organized. Make sure that your address book is up-to-date and that you have a note of all important dates like friends' and family members' birthdays and anniversaries.

- Spend time with as many of your friends as you can manage.

- Catch up with friends you haven't seen for a while – light-hearted chats where you get up to date with the gossip are the order of the day.

- Keep a note of the people you meet casually, together with their contact details so you can look them up in the future.

- Make time for friends when they call, even if this is only five minutes. The pace may feel hectic, but now is the time to nurture your network of contacts.

THINGS TO AVOID

- Don't be disappointed if you just don't feel socially proactive. Different responses to the moon are normal and you may be one of those people who becomes easily overwhelmed during this expansive phase.

- Don't try too hard. The waxing moon encourages opportunities but it does not guarantee success. If someone says 'no', then just move on, giving yourself ten out of ten for being brave enough to try.

- Don't force yourself into situations that you really hate. Give things and people a chance, but be true to yourself, too.

- Don't choose this time to have deep and meaningful conversations unless they are unavoidable. It is better to take constructive action now, rather than search your soul.

- Unless you really have to, this is not the best time to end a relationship. It is likely to be a lot more difficult for one or both of you to let go if there are any feelings left between you.

- Don't stay in on your own unless you have a lot to do or lots of phone calls to make. Even if you are very introverted, you are better off with company during this phase.

- Don't restrict yourself to seeing just one or two best friends, however great they are. You could miss out if you don't socialize a bit more widely.

- Don't expect too much. Not every waxing moon will bring a flood of offers and opportunities. Take things as they come, and one day, one week, one month, what you really want is sure to come floating by.

- Although this is a busy time, there is no need to be involved in everything, with everyone, all the time. If you are too busy, just let some things go. The moon will wax again next month, bringing another tide of opportunity.

LOVE AND RELATIONSHIPS
FULL MOON

During full moon, all of your emotions, both positive and negative, are likely to be strengthened. It is a time of extremes, excitement and fruition, when some of your plans fall into place. However, it can also bring disappointment, when life falls short of your dreams, or when some things turn out not to be viable. This can be tougher to take in the hyped-up climate of the moment. It is hard to be totally sensible at full moon – after all, it is the phase most associated, traditionally, with lunacy! Nothing is likely to turn our heads more than sexual passion, and feelings may also run high in friendships.

This isn't a time for momentous decisions or detailed planning. It is instead a good time for releasing pent-up emotions, so try to let your feelings run their course – whether in tears or laughter. If a display of feeling really may affect things in ways that are not to your long-term benefit, it may be better to distance yourself from the person responsible and unburden yourself to an uninvolved friend. Be careful about being overly confrontational during this phase.

Full moon is an ideal time for celebrations, weddings, engagements and large gatherings of family and friends. By all means, schedule the good times for now but keep in mind that there might be a slightly unpredictable influence around, especially on the actual night of the full moon and the 24 hours on either side of it. This is truly a time of romance and enchantment. We all know relationships involve many practical matters, but now is not the best time to focus on these. Allow yourself to dream and fantasize a little.

THINGS TO DO

- Write down all your thoughts and daydreams in your lunar journal, however bizarre they may seem at first glance. You never know what might come of them.

- Take a day or two off work if you can, to spend some 'quality time' with the people that matter most to you.

- Go on a holiday or a short trip, just for fun.

- Buy someone some flowers.

- Express your feelings to the person that matters, either face to face or in poetry.

- This is a good time to get engaged or married, to make love with a new partner for the first time or to start trying for a baby if that is what you want.

- Have a true 'love fest' with your partner – indulge in all the added extras such as romantic meals, candle-lit baths, oil massages, rose petals scattered on the bed, and champagne and strawberries for breakfast.

- Make love outside, especially in the light of the full moon.

- Dance all night with friends or your lover.

- Buy someone you love an extra-special gift.

- Take a group photo of friends and family, having a wonderful time.

- Make time to play with or tell stories to any children to whom you are close.

- Have a long, indulgent meal with anyone who is special to you.

- Explore mutual interests with your friends and family. Whether you love going bowling or bird-watching, it will be more fun right now.

- Organize a large party with friends and family and serve a 'lunar banquet' of white foods such as grapes, cheese, cucumber, chicken, fish and melon. You may wish to place a large silver candle in the centre of the table in honour of the moon. And you could make or buy some sort of fun, silver-coloured crown and let people take turns at being 'Moon Monarch' – where they give other people light-hearted tasks to do.

THINGS TO AVOID

- It's best not to end a relationship now, unless it is something you've been thinking of doing for a long time and the high emotions of full moon have simply given you the push you have desperately needed.

- Don't let a friend down now – it is likely to hurt them more deeply, and they will not forget it.

- Don't go into situations that you know are likely to upset you, for example, this is not the time to go to a party where you know there's a chance of running into your ex with their new partner.

- Don't spend time with anyone who annoys you or makes you feel bad in any way.

- Try not to go over the past in your mind, re-living old situations, unless the memories are positive and can be shared by other people around you.

- Now can be a good time to get everything out in the open but don't go overboard, as things could easily get out of control.

- It's not worth even telling little white lies during this lunar phase as you run a high risk of being caught out or even giving yourself away.

- This is definitely no time to cheat on a loved one, as the moon sees all!

- Try not to take things too personally, but if you do get upset, take some time alone or find someone you can talk to who is not involved in the situation. It is very easy to get things out of proportion now.

- Don't get too disappointed if things don't work out just as you planned. In a few days it won't seem so bad, anyway.

- Don't try too hard to focus on the practical and sensible aspects of relationships – you may become impatient.

LOVE AND RELATIONSHIPS
WANING MOON

As the moon wanes, you will probably feel less and less like seeking company or making the effort to meet new people. Of course, you will still want to be with the people that matter to you, and if you are extrovert, plenty of contact will still be important, but if any relationship is less than satisfactory, you will probably wish to pull away from it. Generally, you are unlikely to want to bother with anything that's not meeting your emotional needs. Sometimes the waning moon frees up energy for important relationships, simply because you are no longer prepared to waste your efforts on what seems less important.

It is likely that your awareness of anything that is wrong in a relationship will increase during this phase, and you may find yourself wanting to be totally rid of any contact that is in some way hurtful. For example, if friends are being critical or demanding, you will want to withdraw from them. In the case of a one-to-one relationship with a lover or partner, now is the time you are most likely to feel like ending the relationship, if it has been on your mind.

On the other hand, you will probably want to spend quality time with those whom you cherish, enjoying privacy and quieter pursuits. Staying at home with your partner or meeting up with close friends will feel like a good idea. There is a tendency to want to talk about relationships, which is a good thing, as long as you do not allow yourself to become too negative. At new moon you will have an opportunity to act on any decisions you make.

THINGS TO DO

- Generally decrease your social activity, unless you still feel the need for lots of company for some reason.

- End any relationships that you feel have run their course, but beware of simply doing things as a result of a negative mood.

- Put an end to any unhealthy patterns that have developed in your relationships with others. For instance, if someone is mistreating you in any way, take steps to stop this. If you need help, seek it, because although banishing is advised during the waxing moon, you will still need support if you are in a vulnerable position.

- Go through your address book, getting rid of obsolete addresses and contact details.

- Tidy up your social diary. Cancel any dates you have made that you feel are a mistake, for whatever reason.

- Send friends and family cards, recognizing things they have done to help you.

- Reminisce and gossip with old friends.

- Take time to remember old friends, especially loved ones who have passed away. Take flowers to their grave or light a memorial candle. Talk about them with friends and family, and look at old photos.

- Write down things that you remember about the past in your lunar journal. Especially important will be family memories and anything that has left you with strong feelings, whether positive or negative. At dark–new moon, you may then like to take steps to deal with some of these feelings, if you feel it would help you to move forward.

- Expel negative emotions, either by talking them through with friends or with the waning moon exercise on pages 62–63.

- Sort through sentimental gifts, cards and memorabilia relating to old relationships and friendships. Should anything be thrown out? If so, do it.

THINGS TO AVOID

- Don't force yourself to try to make a relationship work when it simply isn't working; use your energies for better things.

- This is not the best time to have a party or major celebration, unless you are happy for it to be somewhat low-key.

- It is best not to try online dating to meet new people during this phase; it may be better to concentrate on old, established friends for now.

- Don't take too many risks in relationships during this phase of the moon. If you aren't quite sure about someone or you do not know if you can trust them, wait a while before taking them into your confidence.

- Don't risk asking someone new out on a date unless there is a particularly good rapport between you.

- Try not to let yourself become too negative. This is a time for paring down and expelling what is not working. It is not a time for being critical of yourself and others.

- Don't get so carried away with getting rid of things that it takes over and you never go out.

- Don't make big changes in any relationship, unless you have thought about it well in advance or you have no choice. This may not be the best time to decide to move in together, for instance.

- It is important not to allow yourself to become fearful or suspicious of new things in light of all this inwardness.

THROUGH THE MOON SIGNS

ARIES

When the moon is in Aries be aware that it can be particularly difficult to see other people's points of view. It is also possible to almost forget a relationship is there, as both parties are so busy pursuing their individual goals. Feelings are very ardent at the moment. Those who are deeply in love will have some very passionate episodes. Friends may declare they are 'best friends' and champion each other vehemently against opposition. Things that are irritating about people close to you will seem even worse under Aries. Those seeking a partner are likely to take more risks and be more impulsive under an Aries moon, and committed singles are likely to go their own way more determinedly.

TAURUS

Even with a waxing moon, this is not the best time for any big changes in relationships, except in the direction of greater stability.

Taurus moon is very sensual, so established lovers may want to indulge in a languid love fest, new sweethearts may find it very easy to progress to physical intimacy and friends may be more tactile with each other, hugging each other, giving massages and similar. Money issues may be discussed and settled in relationships at this time. People who are on their own may feel very much like seeking physical contact. However, relationships are likely to start fairly slowly with a Taurus moon.

GEMINI

This is a good moon for flirting, so you stand a good chance of meeting lots of prospective partners. There may be temptation to play the field a little and to change your mind very quickly in terms of how you feel about a person. Friends are likely to be very chatty and gossipy. Those who live alone may spend lots of time on the phone, arranging dates, or on the internet, taking part in chat-rooms. It is best to make notes of dates and contact details, to be sifted through at a quieter time.

CANCER

Emotional needs are to the fore under a Cancer moon, so quality time with old friends, family and other loved ones is favoured. It is a good moon during which to discuss starting a family, or setting up a home together, especially if the moon is waxing or full. If you cry easily, however, Cancer moon may see you dissolving into tears at the slightest thing. Any new relationship that starts now is also likely to focus on emotional needs. It is most pleasant now to be at home, inviting friends round or spending time alone with your lover, but everyone should be careful not to get too moody.

LEO

Partners may be prone to be wrapped up in their own selfish concerns under a Leo moon. However, if you are proud of your lover, this is a great couple of days to show them off! By the same token, the lunar vibe encourages singles to strut their stuff in order to impress potential partners. It is a time of lavish parties and flamboyant gestures but beware of power struggles. Those who

have strong personalities may be especially strident, and while quieter souls may feel overwhelmed, they may still rebel. Although arguments are likely, there is a lot of warmth around to make up for it.

VIRGO

This is a good time to analyse relationships, so friends and lovers may become critical of each other, or of themselves. In friendships, the accent is likely to be on practical help. If you would like to start a new relationship, you may feel shy and hesitant: do not be surprised if it takes a while to get going. If you are on your own you may feel more picky than usual about what you want in a potential partner. In all cases, it will seem important to get the details right, and any arrangements are likely to be discussed more closely than usual.

LIBRA

This is a wonderful time to go dancing, have a special dinner for two or do anything involving culture and beauty. Established lovers are likely to want to talk about their relationship, seeking greater understanding. Friends are advised to seek even greater rapport and to reach agreement in everything. Anyone who has had a falling out can make peace under this moon. Playing cupid is also a possibility, as is trying online dating or going out on a first date. It is a wonderful time for getting engaged, getting married or moving in together. It is a partnership moon par excellence, when all elements of one-to-one relating are favoured.

SCORPIO

There is a danger that some negative feelings could surface at this time, such as jealousy, possessiveness and suspicion. Any temptation to go through a lover's belongings should be resisted. Established lovers may enjoy some very intense times, and people in new relationships are likely to have a feeling of 'this thing is bigger than the both of us'. It is a time to reveal your intimate secrets, but with great care. Friends may be involved in issues of loyalty, either positively or negatively: jealousy and manipulation are just as possible as self-sacrifice and courage. From the point of view of relationships, this may be the most difficult of the moons, but nonetheless, many changes can be for the positive, clearing the way for better things ahead.

SAGITTARIUS

The feeling around is likely to be 'nothing ventured, nothing gained', so be confident. For example, it's a great time to ask a new person on a date. Friends should have a laugh together under a Sagittarius moon, although there is a thoughtful side to this time, too. Both friends and lovers will want to be aware of the meaning in their association – where it is going and how it is helping each of the parties to progress as an individual. Adventurous and energetic love-making is favoured, and you may be very impulsive. The Sagittarius moon is the best moon to make a commitment, because drawbacks seem manageable and good things plentiful.

CAPRICORN

If you are happy alone, then Capricorn moon will intensify this, but if you are gregarious, you could feel isolated. You may not feel like asking a new contact out on a date, feeling sure you will be turned down, but it's best to give yourself that extra push you need if you are sure you want to be in a relationship with the person. It's not the best time, however, to start something new and exciting. If you are in an established relationship, you may want to discuss pragmatic details and put things on a permanent footing. This is a good moon for commitment and being practical. Old friends and relationships that have stood the test of time are likely to be most valued now, and it is a good time to discharge duties and speak of the past.

AQUARIUS

Anyone who has trouble with close involvement will be more prone to need their freedom now. Relationships can break under this moon if one party makes too many emotional demands. Relationships where the friendship element is strong may be strengthened even more, however. This is a good time to try anything different, so you may find yourself attracted to someone who isn't usually your 'type' or feel like using a fun approach to asking someone out on a date. Friends are likely to feel especially aware of their shared ideals. This is a truthful moon that can be used to clear the air nicely.

PISCES

If you are in an established relationship, as much effort as possible should be put into making it magical now. If you are on your own, you may be especially prone to fantasies about your ideal partner, but there is also a possibility of having a strong, and correct, intuition about someone and it could be hard to tell which is which. This is a wonderful moon for empathy and crying on the shoulder of a trusted friend. Misunderstandings are possible, so check all arrangements and be prepared to laugh if things go wrong.

HOME AND GARDEN
DARK MOON—NEW MOON

The privacy of your home will feel especially valuable at this introspective time, and you will want to feel peaceful and safe, so draw the curtains on the world outside while you relax. Curling up with a good book by the fire seems like a particularly good idea. Likewise your garden will be a haven, and you will enjoy the tranquillity that comes from being close to nature. Growth in your garden will probably be slower at dark moon, bringing a restful atmosphere.

New DIY tasks and projects in the garden are unlikely to appeal to you right now as it seems impossible to get up enough enthusiasm to get going on them. You prefer to relax around your home, doing small things and daydreaming. If you have been thinking about moving house, this phase will probably make you less proactive, although you may feel even more conscious of your own home's shortcomings.

This isn't a completely fallow time, however. New ideas about your home will come to you, and, at new moon, you will begin to visualize improvements. Spend some time just observing what needs doing and getting in tune with what you really want in your surroundings. Gather information about any issues to do with your home, from the practicalities of DIY to your options if you wish to move. Tidy up any issues left over from the last waning moon, when you may well have had a thorough sort-out. Soon you will feel much more like making changes, and the ideas you have now will enable this.

THINGS TO DO

- Spend time in your home, noticing how you feel in each of the rooms. What pleases you? What would you like to change? Try to look at your home as if you were a stranger, so you can be clearer about its features.

- Make a list in your lunar journal of all the things that you would like to do around the house and garden.

- Gather brochures, DIY magazines, fabric samples for curtains and carpets, and colour charts for the walls in line with what you most want to change. Look at these in a relaxed fashion, playing around with ideas.

- Find out the contact details of well-respected builders, carpenters, painters and decorators, if you are even considering having any work done.

- Complete minor cleaning jobs, such as dusting and vacuuming.

- Make sure that all of the household bills are paid and up to date.

- A lack of energy may make you feel like cooking meals that need little preparation, or just using food from the freezer.

- Tidy bookcases, shelves, wardrobes and cabinets that do not need any major sorting.

- Put belongings that you no longer use regularly, but wish to keep, away in the loft or cellar.

- Consider having a feng shui expert assess the energy-balance of your home.

- Try to get your children to bed a little earlier if possible, with a good story to help them sleep, as this is a good time to catch up on sleep.

- If you had a big sort-out at waning moon, make sure you have gotten rid of all the rubbish by new moon.

- Dispose of all garden waste before new moon.

- Spray any plants or trees that may be affected by pests to keep them under control.

- You may wish to cut timber and chop wood for indoor fires or barbecues.

THINGS TO AVOID

- It is best not to have a major sort-out during this phase of the moon – make sure this is finished before the new moon appears.

- Don't start any major new projects such as decorating or renovating – your enthusiasm may not last to see the project through to the end.

- Similarly, it's best not to start any major garden projects at this time, such as landscaping, laying turf or building a pond or swimming pool.

- Don't engage a builder or plumber quite yet if you have plans for work to be done – give yourself time to think.

- It is not advisable to buy furniture, or order a new carpet or curtains at dark moon, as you may soon change your mind about what you want.

- On a similar note, it's best not to buy garden furniture, large toys for children (such as a swing or trampoline) or substantial items for pets, such as a kennel.

- It's best not to try complicated new recipes or organizing large dinner parties at dark moon if possible as you may not feel very inspired.

- It is advisable not to plant seeds of any description during the period of time approaching dark moon, as it is not a time for optimum growth. Instead, wait for a couple of days after dark moon, when the moon is new.

- It is best not to repot houseplants or graft plants or trees during this time.

- Be careful not to over-water or over-feed plants as they will not absorb a lot of water during this lunar phase.

- Don't fertilize the soil during this period as it will not be absorbed well right now.

- It is not advisable to transplant fruit and vegetables during this phase as they may not cope with the transition very well.

- It is traditionally advised not to harvest herbs or vegetables when very close to dark moon.

WAXING MOON

Energy and enthusiasm now increase by the day and you will want to get going with all those plans and schemes you thought up for your home at dark moon. It is a good idea to buy new things to make your living area brighter and to enhance the ambience. You no longer feel you have to put up with what you don't like and you can see clear ways to make the necessary changes. However, you may not be very patient! Try to accept that there are bound to be challenges and obstacles in the path of every DIY project, even when the moon is waxing. If you have been thinking of moving house, now is the time to take action.

Things are likely to shift along faster as the moon waxes, and you may be swept up by the opportunities that present themselves to you. Children and pets are likely to be more energetic in this phase, which may make it harder to keep things tidy and organized. And you are likely to have more interaction with your neighbours.

This is also a very active time in the garden. Plant growth is accelerating and moisture is absorbed in increasing volume. There will be lots for you to do and, if you are a keen gardener, you will be feeling very inspired. Likewise in the kitchen, this may be a time of experimentation. Be prepared to embrace this innovative and inventive phase of the moon by trying anything that appeals, as there is potential for you to enhance all aspects of your home life.

THINGS TO DO

- Start any major renovations you want to do in your home, such as building an extension or converting the loft.

- Also take this opportunity to do any substantial redecorating you have been dreaming about and to tackle any major work that is needed, such as installing a new central-heating system.

- Contact estate agents if you want to buy, sell or rent out your home.

- Buy any new pieces of large furniture you want, such as a bed, sofa or a dining table and chairs.

- It is also a good time to buy large electrical items, such as a new hi-fi system, television or washing machine.

- Revamp the lighting in your home if you feel the need, so that all is bright and illuminated.

- Complete all plumbing jobs and electrical work before full moon if possible.

- Repot houseplants, taking care not to disturb the roots, and water them well.

- Try as many new recipes as you can, using fresh ingredients – produced locally if possible. Keep a record of how this went in your lunar journal.

- Allow children to stay up a little later and spend some quality time with them if possible, as they may not sleep so well if forced to go to bed early during this phase. Make a note of their reaction in your lunar journal.

- Make sure pets get even more exercise than normal and notice how they behave – you may write this up too if you like.

- Plant all seeds of herbs and flowers, and all leafy vegetables that produce above ground as soon as possible after new moon.

- Move cuttings and seedlings of all descriptions from their germinating trays to the garden as they will take to it better now.

- Pick any garden produce that you are going to eat immediately.

- Take on any garden projects you have been thinking about, such as building a wall, a new patio or garden paths.

- Purchase any large items for the garden that you desire, such as patio furniture, a barbecue or a statue or sundial.

THINGS TO AVOID

- Don't get so carried away with all your projects that you bite off more than you can chew. This is a danger when the moon is waxing and could make you irritable if you aren't careful.

- Don't take any chances. If you are working with electricity, make sure you turn it off at the mains. If you are working with plumbing, turn off the water, and if you are climbing a ladder, get someone to hold it.

- Don't be too quick to assume that you are on the way to a quick house-move because things seem to be moving swiftly at first. Things can change quickly, so remain calm and patient.

- It is best not to have a major clear-out during this phase, even if everything seems to be piling up around you. Your energies are best focused on doing more constructive things now – creating rather than eliminating.

- Try not to do too much cleaning or general tidying, such as hand-washing, shampooing carpets or cleaning windows. This is a time for more imaginative exploits.

- It is best not to plant root vegetables or trees at this time as they take more time to root, which is not ideal in this quick-pace phase of the moon.

- Don't lay fertilizer on your garden or mow the lawn just yet.

- Don't prune your plants, for their moisture content is rising. Likewise with timber – do not cut it just yet.

- Don't spend too much time weeding, for the weeds are likely to grow back quicker than you can remove them.

- Don't try to dry produce, such as herbs or flowers, as this is a time of increased moisture.

- Don't pick fruit for bottling, preserving or freezing as it probably will not have reached full fruition as yet.

HOME AND GARDEN
FULL MOON

Naturally, you will not make huge changes in your home during every one of the lunar cycles. You will often only set out to accomplish relatively minor things, but even then, planning and acting in tune with the lunar cycle is likely to make these things run more smoothly. Similarly, many large projects take much more than a month to complete, but observing the rhythm of building up and clearing away to some degree throughout this is likely to make jobs go more smoothly.

At full moon, at least some of your creative projects – whether big or small – are likely to be nearing fruition and there should be something to appreciate and feel good about, so stop and reward yourself a little. You may find yourself wanting to be out socializing more, or you may want to entertain groups of people. If the weather is good, you will be especially keen to take advantage of the moonlit evenings in your garden, if you have one. Whatever you have done or are doing, you will want it to be beautiful and to have that little bit of magic.

Full moon can, however, also make you feel quite restless, so beware that you may start to think that what you have done is not good enough. Things can sometimes move in an unexpected direction at full moon, but do not abandon all your good work as a result of this; it may just be that you have to set it aside for a while and come back to it later. One thing you can be sure of: the lunar cycle will return and if you learn from what has happened, more satisfaction will result in the future.

THINGS TO DO

- This is a good time to collect the key to a new home, if possible.

- Buy carpets, curtains and soft furnishings to make your home look as lovely as possible. New bedding is an especially good purchase, as the full moon is a time for the sweetest dreams.

- Leave the TV off for a night or two to allow your imagination to flourish during this inspirational time.

- Choose special ornaments or pictures to complement the decor.

- Move the furniture around so that you have a change of outlook.

- Leave the curtains open so that the full moon can shine in through the windows, if possible. Record in your journal how this feels.

- Fill your home with special fragrances that are associated with the moon, such as jasmine, lilies and white roses.

- Fill your home with flowers, especially white ones, as they will help bring the lunar vibrations into your home.

- Cook a meal for friends and family using recipes you have been practising at waxing moon.

- Introduce the theme of water into your living space with a water-related ornament or picture or even a fish tank.

- Play your favourite music at full moon to raise the vibrational tone of your home.

- Install a new water feature in your garden, such as a pond or a fountain, as water is the element associated with the moon.

- Children may be at their most active, so play games with them and let them stay up quite late.

- Pets, too, are likely to reach their peak energy point, so make sure you take them out for regular walks and allow them to run free.

- Purchase garden gnomes, wind chimes and other garden ornaments with a magical flavour.

- Add fertilizer to your garden close to full moon in order to let it seep into the ground as the moon wanes.

- Water your garden liberally as plants will absorb moisture quickly during this phase.

- Plant fruit-bearing bushes and, if the weather has been dry, plant seeds.

THINGS TO AVOID

- Don't do major work on the plumbing in your house at full moon if you can avoid it, because floods and burst pipes are more likely.

- On a similar note, try not to leave the washing machine on when you leave the house.

- Don't do any major electrical work either. Full moon can be an unstable time and it is better not to take risks.

- It's best not to do anything around the house that involves an element of danger, such as working on the roof, as accidents and unexpected happenings are more likely now.

- Don't make any major decision regarding a house-move or large-scale home projects for a day or two, because the lunar climate isn't steady enough for you to be sure what will be right.

- Don't throw out too many belongings during this phase. You may not be thinking clearly and could end up regretting what you have done.

- It's important not to lose your temper with or speak harshly to your neighbours, as feelings tend to run high at this time and what you do is likely be remembered.

- Don't start any major cleaning, clearing or sorting at the moment because you are liable to be more disorganized than usual and to get bored quickly.

- Do not prune bushes or cut back plants that you value as they are unlikely to grow back much in the waning phase to come.

- Don't pick produce that you intend to dry and store, as the current lunar rhythm is not conducive to shrinkage.

- Don't do too much weeding in the garden and avoid using weed killers, as full moon is no time for destruction.

- Don't cut timber or chop wood unless you absolutely must as it will be too moist.

- Don't stick to the same food all the time in the kitchen or the same dull routine – variety is the spice of life.

HOME AND GARDEN
WANING MOON

You are unlikely to have the same energy and enthusiasm for major household projects as at waxing or full moon, but a waning moon does not necessarily cause you to feel tired and disinterested in your home. On the contrary, you may feel somehow liberated from the larger demands and able to see the practical things more clearly. You may feel under less pressure to complete everything or to do everything perfectly, which means that you are able to slow down somewhat and focus on a different kind of job, involving sorting things and cutting back.

If you have been putting off clearing out a particular room in your house, for example, waning moon may put you in just the right mood to tackle it. If some things in your creative projects haven't been working out, full moon may have seen you quite emotional and frustrated; with a waning moon, however, you are likely to feel more able to face facts, work out what isn't working well and clear the way for reassessment at dark moon and the development of something better at new moon.

If you have unresolved practicalities, sort these out before returning to the more creative aspects of your life with renewed vigour, with the next new moon. Even if your house is generally tidy and well-ordered, the accent now is still on reducing clutter to a minimum, and letting go of the old to allow room for the new – at new moon.

THINGS TO DO

- Ask yourself what needs sorting in your home. This may be a drawer or closet, or something much larger, such as your loft or cellar. Even if you do not have time to complete the task in this lunar phase, it will give you the necessary impetus to begin. The next waxing moon may then bring new storage solutions.

- Throw out all unwanted items from the house and garden.

- Take lots of old belongings to garage sales or charity shops.

- Buy small items to help you store and sort, such as a rack for CDs or DVDs, a desk-tidy or drawer-dividers.

- Clean your house as thoroughly as you want, not forgetting to move your furniture to tackle dusty corners.

- Resolve all practical matters in and around the house, such as cleaning windows and bathroom tiles, clearing drains and gutters, shampooing carpets, sending curtains to the cleaners and washing the bedding.

- Set yourself free by getting rid of any objects that you have been keeping out of duty, such as an ornament that you hate but haven't thrown out because it was a present.

- Tend to your garden during this time of banishing all things negative by clearing weeds, mowing the lawn, pruning plants, cutting back hedges, thinning out seedlings, sweeping paths and clearing out sheds.

- Harvest produce for long-term storage, such as apples and potatoes, as well as anything that is going to be dried for later use, such as herbs or certain flowers.

- Dig herb roots and cut leaves and bark for use in teas or as medicine, as now is a time of drawing in and cutting back.

- Encourage children to go to bed earlier, as they are likely to have less energy during this phase.

THINGS TO AVOID

- It is best not to start major renovation or redecoration in the home now, but if you really feel the need to, then concentrate on the preparation, such as stripping away previous paint or lifting the old carpet.

- Don't buy major appliances or large items of furniture now, unless you decided on these earlier and have been waiting for the order.

- It is not advised to buy expensive, non-essential items such as paintings or china vases, unless you have wanted them for a long time. Your tastes may not be at their optimum at the moment, so you may change your mind about your purchase later.

- It's best not to put your house on the market during this phase.

- Don't plant seeds or plant out seedlings, especially when it is very close to dark moon.

- It is advised not to harvest fruit and vegetables for immediate consumption unless they are going to go to waste otherwise.

- Make sure you don't over-water your garden or houseplants because water uptake will be reduced during this phase. The exception to this is in extremely dry climates or dry spells.

- It's best not to take on any large garden projects at this time. Small repairs are a different matter though – they are ideal to do now.

- Avoid making large purchases for the garden, such as patio sets or climbing frames. Smaller items such as nets to protect plants or canes for climbing plants are more the order of the day.

THROUGH THE MOON SIGNS

ARIES

Your energy and enthusiasm will be great under an Aries moon, so focus on something that is going to be productive. Jobs that are connected to your roof, such as tiling and chimneys are favoured, but it is essential that adequate safety precautions are taken. Install smoke alarms and take special care with indoor fires. Add something bright to your home by buying curtains and soft furnishings in vibrant reds and oranges. Purchases of iron and steel, and cutting equipment such as kitchen knives, saws, shears and lawn mowers are favoured.

TAURUS

The accent is on your garden and if you have any talent at all for growing things, it will come to the fore under a Taurus moon. Concentrate on nurturing large areas of greenery, such as lawns and hedges. Taurus also delights in flowers and fruits such as roses and apples, so attend to these, too.

Buy a new sofa or bed, invest in luxurious bedding or a deep-pile carpet and treat yourself to some gorgeous cushions in soft, rich fabrics. Colours such as green, rose and gentle blue are ideal. Stock up your refrigerator and enjoy your home. Make sure household bills are paid. Start anything slow-growing and long-term; for example, you could plant a tree.

GEMINI

You may want quick changes in your home under Gemini, as everything can seem boring, but resist the temptation to do anything too drastic! Concentrate on small things such as changing the position of your furniture, putting different cushions on your sofa or moving ornaments or pictures. You may want to buy a new telephone now, as it is an optimum time for effective communication with others. Also attend to magazine racks, stacks of newspapers and IT software, especially anything carrying factual information. Anything modern, light and airy is favoured by Gemini, so buy fabrics in yellow or with interesting prints.

CANCER

Now is a time to love and cherish your home, and your kitchen in particular. Invest in a new stove and make sure that your kitchen cabinets are well-stocked with nutritious goodies for all the family. Pay special attention to anything of sentimental value, give family photos pride of place and make sure that there is enough space for the children to display their achievements. If you have children, this is an especially good time to focus on ways to encourage them to eat healthily. In the garden, it is best to tend to plants such as cucumber and melons, in which the water content is high, and also to plants that have associations with or carry memories from your past. You may also want to introduce water – the element of the moon – in some way to your garden to bring you more in tune with lunar rhythms – perhaps by building a water feature.

LEO

This is a time to be proud of your home and to start projects that make it more impressive, such as landscaping the garden, or repainting large areas. Take particular care of bright or impressive plants, from sunflowers to orange trees. Purchase articles in a gold colour, such as taps or ornaments. The hearth is the heart of the home, so embellish it, and if you have an open fireplace, use it unless the weather is very warm. Have a party to celebrate family achievements and to spend 'quality time' with the children.

VIRGO

Clear away rubbish, and generally tidy and organize everything. Make sure you have adequate bookcases to house your books and proper places for pens, paper, and personal or family administration. All that you buy for your home should be serviceable and do the job for which it is intended, with no raw edges or unfinished details. Look to the therapeutic elements in your home, such as soft furnishings (particularly in gentle greens and browns), but buy vacuum cleaners, brooms and dusters too. Encourage children to catch up with their homework and begin training pets. Pay particular attention to medicinal plants and culinary herbs, as well as to weeding.

LIBRA

You will want your home at its most beautiful, so buy objets d'art and anything purely decorative, and consider refurbishment. Colour harmonizing is favoured now. Your efforts in the garden are best concentrated on flowering plants, especially the most traditionally beautiful, such as roses or peonies. Everywhere you look you will want to see perfection, but since this is not likely to be possible, avoid discontent by making sure that at least one vista offers only what is easy on the eye, and turn your garden chair to face it. You may also want to buy items associated with balance, such as paired items or scales – the zodiac symbol of Libra.

SCORPIO

This is a time for ruthless elimination of anything unwanted in your home and garden, so sort out cluttered cellars and closets, clean out garden ponds and swimming pools, pull out any weeds, and unblock pipes and drains. Deal also with any damp patches and leaks. It is also a deep, often mysterious time, so search for lost objects. Even if you do not find them, you may discover something else long forgotten. Look after root vegetables or anything that requires deep digging, install a burglar alarm if you don't already have one, and take special care that your curtains afford you the privacy you desire.

SAGITTARIUS

Spend as much time as you can outside – this is a good time to play games on the lawn with the children. Think big, but make sure changes will not require sustained effort. For instance, this would be a wonderful time to plant a majestic tree, such as an oak, or to buy a large and exotic Indian rug for the living room, but it would not be so great for setting down a large area of turf or laying your own wall-to-wall carpet. Bring a flavour of other cultures into your home, and opt for daring purple and wine colours. Be adventurous, but remember this is an impulsive and changeable lunar influence.

CAPRICORN

Under Capricorn moon, you will be mainly concerned with security and practical matters. Check your mortgage and insurances are up-to-date and that the locks in your home work well. Cook familiar, traditional food for the family and encourage children to help you with the household chores. Traditional styles and darker colours are favoured. You will want to have control over your domestic situation, but may find that you get in your own way if you try too hard. In the garden, anything that involves stonework is advised. For example, you may wish to build or repair walls and lay paths. Take particular care of plants that have deep roots, and get rid of stubborn weeds, such as dandelions, once and for all.

AQUARIUS

Open all your windows for a while, even if it is chilly, in order to renew and revitalize the air in your home. Try or buy something different for a change, especially if it is an electrical gadget. For example, you could buy a juicer for the kitchen or a new computer for the study. Buy unusual ornaments and try new colour schemes as this is a time for freedom and an element of rebellion. Care for all leafy plants, especially trees; encourage job-sharing with the children; and be prepared to carry out tasks at odd times – why not water the garden at midnight under the full Aquarian moon in August?

PISCES

You may long for a totally different, ideal home, such as a rose-covered cottage or a fantastic penthouse suite. However, as this may be unlikely to happen, concentrate instead on introducing small details of enchantment, rather than doing 'boring' DIY. Light candles, burn essential oils, arrange beautiful but unusual flowers, hang crystals at the window and arrange beautiful glass objects in striking places. You may even wish to install a fish tank in your living room to introduce Pisces' water element. It is also a good idea to stock up the drinks cabinet and invite close friends for an intimate evening in. Play 'let's pretend' with the children to encourage the imaginative vibe of this sign, and look after watery plants or build an outdoor pond.

DARK MOON — NEW MOON

Try not to be negative and despondent about your career and financial situation at dark moon, for it is all too easy only to see what you have not achieved and forget all about the many good things that you have done. Instead, try to be honest with yourself about your successes and shortcomings, and about your goals in life. This is not a phase for much activity, except for projects that have already been set in motion. Instead, it is about reflection and planning.

It is sensible to gather as much information as you can at this stage of the month in order to make future plans. Remember, you do not have to accept your lot without question. You have the power to make changes, take control of your finances and build a better future for yourself, so start looking for ways to do this. You do not have to come up with a master plan – only some ideas to take you further along your route. Make sure you take into account your key strengths and abilities. Often we forget the things we can do well, because they come so easily to us, instead focusing on the factors that challenge us. However, the best way to make money is invariably by doing the things that we like and excel at.

Look back over the past, not with the intention of regretting mistakes and missed opportunities, but with the intention of learning from them. No 'mistake' is truly a mistake if it teaches you something about yourself and life. Make a resolution that you will use this knowledge over the coming month.

THINGS TO DO

- Think carefully about all the things that you are less than contented with in your career and financial affairs. Make a note of these in your lunar diary.

- Make a list of your talents and achievements. If you are feeling negative, ask a friend to remind you of some of these.

- Make a list of your long- and short-term career and financial goals, thinking about how you can best achieve them as you write.

- Plan the coming lunar month, day by day, in an ordinary diary. Make sure that each day you have something to do, however small, that takes you one step closer to one of your goals, even if this is only buying a newspaper or asking a friend for a contact number.

- If there are things and people in your current job that make you less than happy, think about how you can tackle this to make it better.

- If you think that you deserve an increase in salary, plan how you are going to ask for and justify this.

- Gather information and brochures about courses and training organizations that may have something to offer you.

- Be realistic about what you are prepared to give up, albeit temporarily, to further long-term goals. For example, if you want to retrain in a new area of expertise, you may have to take a drop in salary for a few years.

- Gather information about worthwhile bank accounts, investments and insurance policies.

- Review your personal budgeting. Is it working? How might it be improved?

- If you have debts, consider whether there are better ways for you to manage them. How are you going to reduce them?

- Think about reviewing your savings or pension plan. What might work better for you?

THINGS TO AVOID

- It's best not to commit yourself to major changes of career until the waxing moon is properly established.

- It's advisable not to enrol on a training course, unless you have taken time in the previous lunar month to find out that it is truly what you want.

- Do not buy property or make investments at dark moon, unless these have been put into motion earlier in the lunar month.

- Do not confront a colleague, manager, customer or anyone else related to your career about their shortcomings or things they have done to upset you. Instead, think carefully about how you will handle this at a later point in the month.

- Don't make any major purchases unless they have long been intended.

- It is not advisable to ask for an increase in your salary just yet.

- Don't commit yourself to a savings plan that demands you invest a set amount or that does not give you access to your money for an extended period. At the moment, your assessment of your regular needs may be less than what is required and you could leave yourself short.

- Try not to give in to negative thinking or allow yourself to focus on your faults and the things you have failed at. It is natural to reflect on the past occasionally, but now is a time to focus on the future and what you can and will do.

- Do not aim too low. Identify what you really want and aim even higher. You can always adjust your sights later on if it proves necessary.

- Be realistic in your personal budgeting. You may think you can make do with less than you really can. Don't forget you need to allow money for treats too!

CAREER AND FINANCES
WAXING MOON

It is not surprising that the waxing moon stimulates expansion in career matters. It is therefore time to act on the career plans you have formulated and the information you have gathered at dark moon. You will probably have more energy and determination now, and while the waxing moon will not make an instinctively shy person more confident, you can learn to take advantage of the lunar influence to find ways to at least look as though you have increased confidence.

Naturally, opportunities occur for advancement at all of the lunar phases but they are likely to be more abundant and noticeable now if you keep your eyes open. That means that it's more important now than ever to think positively. Needless to say, not everything that looks good will come to fruition, but remind yourself that everything you do will teach you – both about yourself and the world around you.

Traditionally, this is also a time to make your money grow, so take any necessary action to increase your wealth. Unless finance is your profession, by no means every waxing moon will call on you to make major financial decisions and investments. However, you should ride with the lunar tide while it is on the increase if you

can. Try to keep a relaxed and playful attitude, for then you will be in a better frame of mind to notice opportunities. Research has shown that lucky people are those who are observant and have an optimistic, cheerful outlook. Keep a smile on your face to get the best of the waxing moon.

THINGS TO DO

- Consult your diary each morning. What task are you due to do today to take you closer to your goals, according to the schedule you drew up during dark moon? Make sure you carry it out, or if this is impossible, reschedule it for another day.

- Try not to miss any opportunities. Give yourself time, at the end of each day, to think over what has happened. Were there any openings that you did not follow up? Make a note to chase them up the next day.

- Update and revamp your CV.

- Read self-help books in your free time and try to put into practice one or two things that are likely to develop your character and bring increased success.

- You should apply now for any training courses and evening classes that you have decided would be to your advantage.

- Ask for an increase in salary or a promotion if you feel you deserve it. If this is not forthcoming, ask for feedback on why not in order to establish how you might be successful in the future.

- If you are unhappy about a situation at work, make your feelings known to those that matter, but be sure to choose your words carefully.

- Apply for a new job if you feel so inclined. It is fine to put in several applications to different companies at once to see what comes to fruition.

- This is an ideal time to open a new bank account, commit yourself to a regular savings plan, take out a well-considered loan or make wise investments.

- Waxing moon is the best time to make major purchases of any kind.

- Keep your spirits high by writing three good things that have happened to you each evening in your journal, however small they might seem.

THINGS TO AVOID

- Try not to be too rash or impatient at this stage. It is better to use the forward motion of this lunar phase to put into practice what you thought through at dark moon, not to rush off in a completely new direction.

- Try not to be too demanding or pushy. Healthy self-assertion means being judicious and relaxed.

- Don't over-commit yourself financially. Again, anything you do should have been thoroughly worked out in advance.

- Don't turn down opportunities, even if they do not seem to be leading anywhere at first. Meet as many people as you can and visit as many places as possible, as you never know what might come of this later. Yes, this is a busy time but you know that it won't last forever.

- It's best not to leave the office early, take long lunches or start work late in the day. Now is the time for tackling a large workload and getting ahead of schedule if possible.

- This is not a time to leave the phone off the hook. If your concentration is continually interrupted, keep a notepad beside you and write everything down as you do it. It is better taking the time to do this than missing a valuable phone call that could cause you to miss out on something lucrative.

- Don't expect your work to keep to the same routine – be flexible.

- Don't turn down a bargain as long as you're sure that it really is a good deal. Try to buy yourself time to think if you need it, and if you are making a purchase, ensure you can get a refund if necessary.

- Aim not to talk in negatives. Speak about what you can do rather than what you cannot.

- Don't scatter your efforts or spread yourself too thin. There is a fine line between making the most of all opportunities and simply overloading yourself, so be aware of this.

CAREER AND FINANCES
FULL MOON

Full moon may increase your self-confidence, or at least put you in the sort of mood where you manage to put all your concerns to the side and forge ahead regardless. You can certainly aim high during this phase, but it is a good idea to cultivate a philosophical attitude as it can also bring disappointments. If things are not destined to work out, for example if a job opportunity is not going to come your way or an investment is going to let you down, full moon may be the time when you have to face this fact and begin to let go.

Many matters that you have been working on may come to fruition during this creative and inspired time, when ideas just seem to materialize out of the ether. At work, it is a good time to celebrate commercial or creative successes, and an office party held now is likely to be a riot! Issues may come to light that are less than comfortable, but that could prove useful in the long run.

Intuitions and instincts may be strong at this time, so learn to listen to them. Your energy may be at its height and it may seem that all things are possible. However, it is just as easy to fool yourself at full moon as it is to achieve great things. At its best, full moon can show you totally different perspectives, the value of lateral thinking and even flashes of inspirational genius! However, the line between genius and madness is a thin one, and you may need to remind yourself to keep things in perspective and to be moderate.

THINGS TO DO

- Keep a diary by your bed and make a note of all the thoughts that occur to you when you wake up, the dreams you have had and the impressions that have come to the surface, however strange they may seem. They may hold the key to your future.

- Make a note of all the creative ideas you have and place them in a file or in your lunar diary. At some point, when you have time, you may want to put the best ones into practice.

- Listen to your intuition in all matters. Tune in to your body – how does it feel? Often instincts translate themselves into physical sensations. For instance, is your headache or upset stomach telling you that your latest financial deal or job offer is not so good after all?

- If you are a boss, review your employees' work and achievements, and reward them with a party, a meal out or a small gift of some sort.

- If you are an employee, suggest that you and your colleagues look at what you have achieved and have a small celebration if appropriate.

- Have a brainstorming session with colleagues to see how you could help each other around the office and make the working environment more pleasing to everyone.

- Be prepared to work late into the night to complete a work or study project, if necessary, as your energy is at its peak during this phase of the moon.

- If you have the funds, now is a good time for a spending spree, but have some idea of what you need to buy beforehand or you might become overly self-indulgent.

- Stock up on office essentials if you are in a position to do so – from stationery to tea and coffee supplies – as you can feel legitimate buying these sorts of items, even if the impetus is really you wanting to buy armfuls of stuff.

- As with a waxing moon, this is a good time to make investments and start new financial ventures, but not on impulse.

THINGS TO AVOID

- Don't go over the top with anything financial, for you may not be thinking clearly and practically.

- Don't work too long and hard at anything, as you run the risk of damaging your health.

- Don't try to be too logical. Your train of thought may be disrupted or something unpredictable may intervene.

- Don't allow yourself to be too extravagant, for this is a real danger at full moon. This phase is about letting yourself go a little, but be aware of your limits!

- Try not to let your imagination take hold of you so much that you lose your grip on reality. If you come across a job tailored for you, a great investment to make or a training course that seems perfect for you, it will still be there in a couple of days, when you have had time to think. If not, it mustn't be for you after all!

- Do not reason yourself out of any idea, however outrageous it may seem at first. It may hold the seed of something worthwhile.

- Try not to plan too much. This is a time to be spontaneous and open to some degree, and you could lose out if you are too controlled.

- It's best not to let yourself get too upset by the words and actions of colleagues or by things that don't work out. It is easy to over-react at full moon and this could make things more difficult in the long run.

- Avoid overloading yourself with lists of contacts to make, things to chase up or masses of information about bank accounts, savings, mortgages and so on. It is easy to become overwhelmed by too many practical details during full moon.

- Don't renege on promises you have made – you may never be forgiven!

CAREER AND FINANCES
WANING MOON

As in all other areas of life, activities in your career and finances are likely to decrease with this phase. It may not be that less is happening, exactly, but that the pace slows down, people's attitudes shift and your expectations alter. This is by no means a negative or unlucky phase – quite the contrary. However, the emphasis changes now from increase and fulfilment to toning down and reducing.

This is a good time to move on from things that are not working out and to let go of outworn ideas. This is not a time for guilt and recrimination, or to make yourself feel bad in any way about the things that you have not done, or cannot do at the moment. Instead, it is an opportunity for separating the good from the bad, and learning not to waste time or money.

Paradoxically, some people feel more energy with a waning moon, as if the pressure has been lifted. Certainly it can be a pleasant feeling to be cutting things out of your working life. The same applies to finances. There is always something that can be pared down and now is the time to look for it. Options that you have been exploring since new moon – whether in your job, training courses or financial affairs – will probably have shown their value or otherwise by now, which means you can eliminate the least successful safe in the knowledge that you have tried them. This is all part of the process that will take you forward in life if you learn from it as you go along.

THINGS TO DO

- Even if you are given a deadline, make sure you get plenty of rest during the waning moon. You may run out of steam if you do not, and the quality of your work may deteriorate.

- If you feel you may let people down, warn them in advance and negotiate more time for yourself.

- Review your finances, looking for any areas where you are being wasteful. Waste does no one any good and can often be reduced without cutting down too much on the pleasures of life.

- Cut down on general expenditure. One small way of doing this is by using up what is already in your kitchen cabinets so that you decrease your week's shopping list.

- Sort out your desk and dispose of anything you no longer need or want.

- If you have been unhappy in your job and manage to find a new one that is more to your liking, waning moon is a good time to leave the old job. However, you should take a week off before starting your new role if possible.

- Throw out brochures and information on companies and investments that you have decided not to pursue.

- Try to become aware of office politics by detaching yourself a little from situations and thinking analytically.

- If you are on a training course, tidy up your notes and throw out what you no longer need, to facilitate study.

- Review your investments. Are any of them not giving you the return that you wish for? Be prepared to offload these to make room for something better.

- This may be a time to organize good or better insurance cover or a pension plan, as the waning moon turns our attention to being prepared for reversals in fortune (although it doesn't have to create them).

THINGS TO AVOID

- It's best not to commence any major new financial venture unless you have researched it thoroughly and already sown the seeds.

- Don't abandon your job just because you are in a negative mood or feel you can't cope.

- It's best not to start a new job at this time unless it is absolutely unavoidable.

- Try not to drive yourself too hard during this phase. For example, it's not worth working through your lunch hour or staying late at the office unless this gives you some much-needed peace and privacy.

- Don't abandon routine – it can be an anchor at this phase.

- Try not to give in to fears and negative thoughts. If you think that people are criticizing you behind your back you are probably wrong, and, even if they were, it can only affect your future if you let it.

- Don't beat yourself up over lost opportunities. Something even better will come along if you think positively.

- Don't make any substantial changes to your CV at this time. You may forget to include some of your best assets and achievements.

- Don't try to look too far into the future. 'Sufficient unto the day' is a good motto for this phase of the moon.

- Avoid confronting too many problems at work, as there is a danger that you may be overly negative right now.

- Don't make important purchases that are connected with your job or career, such as a suit for interviews or a new computer, unless these are unavoidable, as you may not be in the best frame of mind to make good decisions.

CAREER AND FINANCES
THROUGH THE MOON SIGNS

ARIES

Get going on any new enterprise, whether it is a new job, a totally new career, a training course or a financial investment. It is a good time for blitzing a pile of work and getting ahead of schedule. However, there is a very strong risk of impulsiveness, especially with a waxing moon. This is not a good time for tying up loose ends, as you may miss something. You could, however, apply for a job or start a training course in any of the following under Aries: butcher, engineer, surgeon, armed forces recruit, dentist, mechanic, engine driver, armaments trader, sword maker, psychiatrist or psychologist.

TAURUS

This stolid, steady lunar influence is best for routine matters, such as keeping accounts up to date, calculating assets and generally attending to the financial affairs of any business or institution. This is the lunar influence par excellence for money matters. Anything to do with creativity or beauty is also a Taurus matter. This could be a suitable time to ask for a salary increase, if you truly think you have earned it. Apply for a job or start a training course in any of the following under Taurus: banking, real estate, accounting, civil service, farming, building, architecture, jewellery trade, antique or art trade, sculpting, art, music, modelling or photography.

GEMINI

When the moon is in Gemini, it is a good time to catch up with correspondence, all the latest news and telephone calls, and to scan newspapers and magazines for job opportunities. It is also a suitable time to have someone explain something to you regarding office systems or similar. You may have to do a variety of tasks and can learn much if you don't gossip. Interaction with other people is favoured. Apply for a job or start a training course in any of the following under Gemini: reporting, writing, journalism, languages and interpreting, sales, broadcasting, teaching, secretarial work, driving or navigating.

CANCER

If you work alone you may feel lonely when the moon is in Cancer. Although you may just feel like staying home with your family, it would be better for you to go out and bond with other people. Personal needs may interfere with work and require attention, so look at how your family experiences are shaping your attitude in your work or training. Apply for a job or start a training course in any of the following under Cancer: nursing, counselling, teaching infants, catering, hotel work, gardening, childminding, caretaking, marine biology, art or antiques.

LEO

This is a time of broad vision, so details may seem annoying and creativity is favoured. Tremendous energy is available and there can be lots of fun at work. There is a feeling that anything is possible, so this could be a good time to start any large-scale ventures you have in mind. Be generous, but be careful not to make the person you

give to feel inferior. For anything that looks half reasonable, it is a time to aim high and play to win. Apply for a job or start a training course in any of the following under Leo: performing arts, stage-craft and theatre, film and media, teaching, youth work, management, the jewellery industry, social organizations or entrepreneurial work.

VIRGO

If anything is wrong, it is likely to surface under a Virgo moon, causing annoyance. Concentrate on organizational structure, systems analysis and anything involving measure and precision. Prioritize jobs and make sure your work area is clean and tidy. Anything second-rate is not likely to be readily tolerated under Virgo moon, so aim to get things absolutely right, even if you accomplish less overall. Apply for a job or start a training course in any of the following under Virgo: editing, proof-reading, secretarial work, computing, clerical work, science, laboratory work, statistics, teaching, gardening, crafts, hygiene, nutrition, psychology, technology, literary criticism or nursing.

LIBRA

Tact, diplomacy and the signing of contracts are favoured under a Libra moon, so avoid anything unfair or underhand. Make your workplace look as pleasant as possible and try to resolve any disputes. Everyone may feel a little lazy when under the Libra influence, but this may give relationships between co-workers a chance to develop. This is a time to invest in the beautiful, but guard against extravagance. Apply for a job or start a training course in any of the following under Libra: diplomatic corps, counselling (especially marriage guidance), beauty therapy, dress design, interior design, hairdressing, welfare work, the law or any luxury business.

SCORPIO

When the moon is in Scorpio, you should take your work seriously and concentrate on fundamentals. You should also sort out life assurance and make a will. Anyone who is at all prone to fears and negative thinking may become a little paranoid during this period. It is therefore a good time for any questionable dealings to be thoroughly investigated. Apply for a job or start a training course in any of the following under Scorpio: surgery, psychoanalysis, research, analysis, detective or police work, armed forces, physics, the meat trade, science, law, the healing therapies, pathology, the pharmaceutical industry or insurance.

SAGITTARIUS

The moon in Sagittarius provides the ideal opportunity for you to make large purchases and investments. Gamble in moderation if you want, and if you don't win... well, better luck next time! If you are on a training course, this is a great time to get well ahead with your work; and if you are thinking of changing your job or becoming self-employed, now's the time to do it. Apply for a job or start a training course in any of the following under Sagittarius: exploring, travel, teaching (especially higher education), academic work, coaching, philosophy, high-level administration, law, religion, language and interpreting, publishing or bookselling – as Sagittarius is a sign of higher mind, philosophy, expanding consciousness and adventure.

CAPRICORN

A moon in Capricorn is a time for you to put your nose to the grindstone and work as hard as you can towards your ambitions. It may be an auspicious time to start a long-term training course or buy land but don't expect quick results. At work, the atmosphere may be somewhat low-key, with everyone concentrating on completing their jobs. It's not a time to change traditional ways of doing things. Apply for a job or start a training course in any of the following under Capricorn: mathematics, building, osteopathy, science, civil service, politics, music, architecture, surveying, administration, management, sculpting or mineralogy – as Capricorn is all about structure and patterns.

AQUARIUS

An Aquarius moon provides a platform for original methods, so choose irregular work shifts if they are optional and install a new computer system now, if you want. Friendliness may abound at this time but teamwork can be difficult as colleagues are likely to focus on their own ideas.

Financial advancement is unlikely to be a motivation, but a mentally stimulating training course may be exciting. Whatever the job, it will go better if you open a window or do as much of it as possible outside, as this is a time for the outdoors. Apply for a job or start a training course in any of the following under Aquarius: science, computing, writing, politics, sociology, charity work, astrology, astronomy, radiography, humanitarian work, work with animals or plants.

PISCES

This is not a time to focus on money matters, unless they are connected to charity or the creative and artistic. There may be considerable rapport among colleagues around now. If you are helping someone or working in music, drama or art, wonderful things can be done. Beware, however, of getting a little lost in it all. Apply for a job or start a training course in any of the following under Pisces: nursing, medicine, charity work, social work, the priesthood, clairvoyance, performing arts, counselling, hypnotism, the navy, photography.

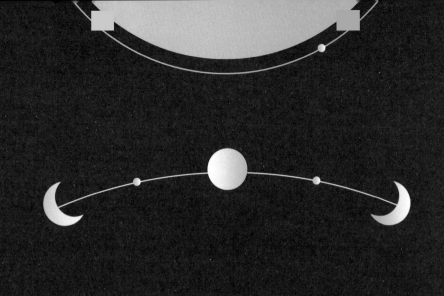

FINDING YOUR
MOON SIGN

STAGE 1

Find the zodiac sign the moon was in at the start of the month when you were born. To do this, look for your year of birth on the left of the table on pages 133–135, then look in the appropriate column under the correct month.

STAGE 2

Now use the zodiac wheel to help you calculate your moon sign. Start at the zodiac sign the moon was in at the start of the month in which you were born, then count back anticlockwise according to the number shown for your date of birth.

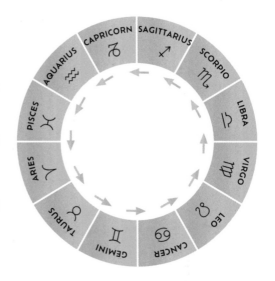

EXAMPLE

Birthday on 9 September 1997.
Step 1: At the start of September 1997 the moon was in ♍.
Step 2: For the 9th, count back three signs. Answer: ♐.
The moon sign for 9 September 1997 is Sagittarius.

NOTE:

The variable nature of the moon's orbit means these tables are only 70 per cent accurate. For a proper birth chart, you are advised to contact an experienced astrologer.

KEY TO SIGNS:

Aries	♈	Libra	♎
Taurus	♉	Scorpio	♏
Gemini	♊	Sagittarius	♐
Cancer	♋	Capricorn	♑
Leo	♌	Aquarius	♒
Virgo	♍	Pisces	♓

NUMBER OF SIGNS TO COUNT BACK

1st	0	12th	4	23rd	9
2nd	0	13th	5	24th	9
3rd	0	14th	5	25th	10
4th	1	15th	6	26th	11
5th	1	16th	6	27th	11
6th	2	17th	6	28th	0
7th	2	18th	7	29th	0
8th	3	19th	7	30th	1
9th	3	20th	8	31st	1
10th	3	21st	8		
11th	4	22nd	9		

Year	Jan	Feb	Mar	Apr	May	June	July	Aug	Sept	Oct	Nov	Dec
1924	♏	♑	♑	♓	♈	♊	♋	♌	♎	♏	♐	♒
1925	♓	♉	♊	♋	♌	♎	♏	♐	♒	♓	♉	♊
1926	♌	♎	♎	♐	♑	♒	♓	♉	♋	♌	♎	♏
1927	♑	♒	♒	♈	♉	♋	♌	♎	♏	♑	♒	♓
1928	♉	♊	♋	♌	♍	♏	♑	♒	♈	♉	♊	♋
1929	♍	♏	♏	♑	♒	♈	♉	♊	♌	♍	♏	♐
1930	♒	♓	♈	♉	♊	♌	♍	♏	♑	♒	♈	♉
1931	♊	♌	♌	♎	♏	♑	♒	♈	♉	♊	♌	♍
1932	♎	♐	♐	♒	♓	♉	♊	♌	♍	♎	♐	♑
1933	♓	♉	♉	♋	♌	♍	♎	♐	♑	♓	♈	♊
1934	♋	♍	♎	♏	♐	♒	♓	♉	♊	♌	♍	♎
1935	♐	♑	♒	♓	♈	♊	♌	♍	♏	♐	♑	♒
1936	♈	♊	♊	♌	♍	♏	♐	♑	♓	♈	♊	♋
1937	♍	♎	♏	♐	♑	♓	♈	♉	♋	♌	♎	♏
1938	♑	♓	♓	♉	♊	♋	♍	♎	♐	♑	♓	♈
1939	♊	♋	♋	♍	♎	♐	♑	♓	♈	♊	♋	♌
1940	♎	♏	♐	♑	♓	♈	♊	♋	♍	♎	♏	♑
1941	♒	♈	♈	♊	♋	♍	♎	♏	♑	♒	♈	♉
1942	♋	♌	♍	♎	♐	♑	♒	♈	♊	♋	♍	♎
1943	♏	♑	♑	♓	♈	♊	♋	♍	♎	♏	♑	♒
1944	♓	♉	♉	♋	♍	♎	♏	♑	♒	♓	♉	♊
1945	♌	♎	♎	♐	♑	♒	♓	♉	♊	♌	♎	♏
1946	♐	♒	♓	♈	♉	♋	♌	♎	♐	♑	♒	♓
1947	♉	♊	♋	♌	♎	♏	♑	♒	♈	♉	♊	♋
1948	♍	♏	♏	♑	♒	♈	♉	♊	♌	♍	♏	♐
1949	♒	♓	♈	♉	♊	♌	♍	♎	♐	♑	♓	♈
1950	♊	♌	♌	♍	♏	♑	♒	♓	♉	♊	♋	♍
1951	♎	♐	♐	♒	♓	♉	♊	♋	♍	♎	♐	♑
1952	♓	♉	♉	♋	♌	♍	♎	♐	♒	♓	♉	♊
1953	♌	♍	♍	♏	♐	♒	♓	♉	♊	♌	♍	♎
1954	♐	♑	♑	♓	♈	♊	♋	♍	♏	♐	♑	♒
1955	♈	♊	♊	♌	♍	♏	♐	♑	♓	♈	♊	♋
1956	♍	♎	♏	♐	♑	♓	♈	♊	♌	♍	♏	♐
1957	♑	♓	♓	♉	♊	♋	♍	♎	♐	♑	♓	♈

Year	Jan	Feb	Mar	Apr	May	June	July	Aug	Sept	Oct	Nov	Dec
1958	♉	♋	♋	♍	♎	♐	♑	♓	♈	♉	♋	♌
1959	♎	♏	♐	♒	♓	♈	♉	♋	♌	♎	♏	♑
1960	♒	♈	♉	♊	♋	♍	♎	♏	♑	♓	♈	♉
1961	♋	♌	♍	♎	♏	♑	♒	♈	♊	♋	♌	♍
1962	♏	♑	♑	♓	♈	♊	♋	♌	♎	♏	♐	♒
1963	♓	♉	♊	♋	♌	♎	♏	♐	♒	♓	♉	♊
1964	♌	♎	♎	♐	♑	♒	♓	♉	♋	♌	♎	♏
1965	♑	♒	♒	♈	♉	♋	♌	♎	♏	♑	♒	♓
1966	♉	♊	♋	♌	♍	♏	♑	♒	♈	♉	♊	♋
1967	♍	♏	♏	♑	♒	♈	♉	♊	♌	♍	♏	♐
1968	♒	♓	♈	♉	♊	♌	♍	♏	♑	♒	♈	♉
1969	♊	♌	♌	♎	♏	♑	♒	♈	♉	♊	♌	♍
1970	♎	♐	♐	♒	♓	♉	♊	♌	♍	♎	♐	♑
1971	♓	♉	♉	♋	♌	♍	♎	♐	♑	♓	♈	♊
1972	♋	♍	♎	♏	♐	♒	♓	♉	♊	♌	♍	♎
1973	♐	♑	♒	♓	♈	♊	♌	♍	♏	♐	♑	♒
1974	♈	♊	♊	♌	♍	♏	♐	♑	♓	♈	♊	♋
1975	♍	♎	♏	♐	♑	♓	♈	♉	♋	♌	♎	♏
1976	♑	♓	♓	♉	♊	♋	♍	♎	♐	♑	♓	♈
1977	♊	♋	♋	♍	♎	♐	♑	♓	♈	♊	♋	♌
1978	♎	♏	♐	♑	♓	♈	♊	♋	♍	♎	♏	♑
1979	♒	♈	♈	♊	♋	♍	♎	♏	♑	♒	♈	♉
1980	♋	♌	♍	♎	♐	♑	♒	♈	♊	♋	♍	♎
1981	♏	♑	♑	♓	♈	♊	♋	♍	♎	♏	♑	♒
1982	♓	♉	♉	♋	♍	♎	♏	♑	♒	♓	♉	♊
1983	♌	♎	♎	♐	♑	♒	♓	♉	♊	♌	♎	♏
1984	♐	♒	♓	♈	♉	♋	♌	♎	♐	♑	♒	♓
1985	♉	♊	♋	♌	♎	♏	♑	♒	♈	♉	♊	♋
1986	♍	♏	♏	♑	♒	♈	♉	♊	♌	♍	♏	♐
1987	♒	♓	♈	♉	♊	♌	♍	♎	♐	♑	♓	♈
1988	♊	♌	♌	♎	♏	♑	♒	♈	♉	♋	♌	♍
1989	♏	♐	♐	♒	♓	♉	♊	♌	♍	♏	♐	♑
1990	♓	♉	♉	♋	♌	♎	♏	♐	♒	♓	♈	♊
1991	♋	♍	♍	♏	♐	♒	♓	♈	♊	♋	♍	♎

Year	Jan	Feb	Mar	Apr	May	June	July	Aug	Sept	Oct	Nov	Dec
1992	♐	♑	♒	♓	♉	♊	♌	♍	♏	♐	♒	♓
1993	♈	♊	♊	♌	♍	♏	♐	♒	♓	♈	♊	♋
1994	♍	♎	♏	♐	♒	♓	♈	♊	♋	♌	♎	♏
1995	♑	♓	♓	♉	♊	♋	♌	♎	♐	♑	♓	♈
1996	♉	♋	♌	♍	♎	♐	♑	♓	♉	♊	♋	♌
1997	♎	♏	♐	♑	♓	♈	♊	♋	♍	♎	♏	♑
1998	♒	♈	♈	♊	♋	♍	♎	♏	♑	♒	♈	♉
1999	♋	♌	♍	♎	♏	♑	♒	♈	♉	♋	♌	♎
2000	♏	♑	♑	♓	♈	♊	♋	♍	♎	♐	♑	♒
2001	♈	♉	♉	♋	♌	♎	♏	♑	♒	♈	♉	♊
2002	♌	♎	♎	♐	♑	♓	♈	♉	♋	♌	♍	♏
2003	♑	♒	♒	♈	♉	♋	♌	♍	♏	♐	♒	♓
2004	♉	♊	♋	♌	♍	♏	♑	♒	♈	♉	♋	♌
2005	♍	♏	♏	♑	♒	♈	♉	♋	♌	♍	♏	♐
2006	♒	♈	♈	♊	♋	♌	♍	♏	♐	♑	♓	♈
2007	♊	♋	♌	♎	♏	♐	♑	♓	♉	♊	♌	♍
2008	♎	♐	♑	♒	♓	♉	♊	♌	♎	♏	♐	♑
2009	♓	♉	♉	♋	♌	♎	♏	♐	♒	♓	♈	♊
2010	♋	♍	♍	♏	♐	♒	♓	♈	♊	♋	♍	♎
2011	♐	♑	♒	♓	♈	♊	♋	♌	♎	♐	♑	♓
2012	♈	♉	♊	♋	♍	♎	♐	♑	♓	♈	♊	♋
2013	♌	♎	♎	♐	♑	♓	♈	♊	♋	♌	♎	♏
2014	♑	♓	♓	♈	♊	♋	♌	♎	♏	♑	♒	♈
2015	♉	♋	♋	♍	♎	♏	♐	♒	♈	♉	♋	♌
2016	♍	♏	♐	♑	♒	♈	♉	♋	♍	♎	♏	♐
2017	♒	♈	♈	♊	♋	♍	♎	♏	♑	♒	♓	♉
2018	♊	♌	♌	♎	♏	♑	♒	♓	♉	♊	♌	♍
2019	♏	♑	♑	♒	♓	♉	♊	♌	♎	♏	♐	♒
2020	♓	♉	♉	♋	♌	♎	♏	♑	♒	♈	♉	♊
2021	♌	♎	♎	♐	♑	♓	♈	♉	♋	♌	♍	♏
2022	♑	♒	♒	♈	♉	♋	♌	♍	♏	♐	♒	♓
2023	♉	♊	♋	♌	♍	♏	♑	♒	♈	♉	♋	♌
2024	♍	♏	♏	♑	♒	♈	♉	♋	♌	♍	♏	♐
2025	♒	♈	♈	♊	♋	♌	♍	♏	♐	♑	♓	♈

LUNAR PHASE TABLES
FOR 2022–2030

KEY TO SYMBOLS IN LUNAR PHASE CHARTS

Aries	♈	Leo	♌	Sagittarius	♐
Taurus	♉	Virgo	♍	Capricorn	♑
Gemini	♊	Libra	♎	Aquarius	♒
Cancer	♋	Scorpio	♏	Pisces	♓

Lunar eclipse ☍

Solar eclipse ☌

1st quarter	Full moon	3rd quarter	New moon
			Jan 2 ♑
Jan 9 ♈	Jan 17 ♋	Jan 25 ♏	Feb 1 ♒
Feb 8 ♉	Feb 16 ♌	Feb 23 ♐	Mar 2 ♓
Mar 10 ♊	Mar 18 ♍	Mar 25 ♑	Apr 1 ♈
Apr 9 ♋	Apr 16 ♎	Apr 23 ♒	Apr 30 ♉ᵈ
May 9 ♌	May 16 ♏ᵈ	May 22 ♓	May 30 ♊
June 7 ♍	June 14 ♐	June 21 ♓	June 29 ♋
July 7 ♎	July 13 ♑	July 20 ♈	July 28 ♌
Aug 5 ♏	Aug 12 ♒	Aug 19 ♉	Aug 27 ♍
Sep 3 ♐	Sep 10 ♓	Sep 17 ♊	Sep 25 ♎
Oct 3 ♑	Oct 9 ♈	Oct 17 ♋	Oct 25 ♏ᵈ
Nov 1 ♒	Nov 8 ♉ᵈ	Nov 16 ♌	Nov 23 ♐
Nov 30 ♓	Dec 8 ♊	Dec 16 ♍	Dec 23 ♑
Dec 30 ♈			

2022

1st quarter	Full moon	3rd quarter	New moon
	Jan 6 ♋	Jan 15 ♎	Jan 21 ♒
Jan 28 ♉	Feb 5 ♌	Feb 13 ♏	Feb 20 ♓
Feb 27 ♊	Mar 7 ♍	Mar 15 ♐	Mar 21 ♈
Mar 29 ♋	Apr 6 ♎	Apr 13 ♑	Apr 20 ♈ᵈ
Apr 27 ♌	May 5 ♏ᵈ	May 12 ♒	May 19 ♉
May 27 ♍	June 4 ♐	June 10 ♓	June 18 ♊
June 26 ♎	July 3 ♑	July 10 ♈	July 17 ♋
July 25 ♏	Aug 1 ♒	Aug 8 ♉	Aug 16 ♌
Aug 24 ♐	Aug 31 ♓	Sep 6 ♊	Sep 15 ♍
Sep 22 ♐	Sep 29 ♈	Oct 6 ♋	Oct 14 ♎ᵈ
Oct 22 ♑	Oct 28 ♉ᵈ	Nov 5 ♌	Nov 13 ♏
Nov 20 ♒	Nov 27 ♊	Dec 5 ♍	Dec 12 ♐
Dec 19 ♓	Dec 27 ♋		

2023

1st quarter	Full moon	3rd quarter	New moon
		Jan 4 ♎	Jan 11 ♑
Jan 18 ♈	Jan 25 ♌	Feb 2 ♏	Feb 9 ♒
Feb 16 ♉	Feb 24 ♍	Mar 3 ♐	Mar 10 ♓
Mar 17 ♊	Mar 25 ♎☍	Apr 2 ♑	Apr 8 ♈☌
Apr 15 ♋	Apr 23 ♏	May 1 ♒	May 8 ♉
May 15 ♌	May 23 ♐	May 30 ♓	June 6 ♊
June 14 ♍	June 22 ♑	June 28 ♈	July 5 ♋
July 13 ♎	July 21 ♑	July 28 ♉	Aug 4 ♌
Aug 12 ♏	Aug 19 ♒	Aug 26 ♊	Sep 3 ♍
Sep 11 ♐	Sep 18 ♓☍	Sep 24 ♋	Oct 2 ♎☌
Oct 10 ♑	Oct 17 ♈	Oct 24 ♌	Nov 1 ♏
Nov 9 ♒	Nov 15 ♉	Nov 23 ♍	Dec 1 ♐
Dec 8 ♓	Dec 15 ♊	Dec 22 ♎	Dec 30 ♑

2024

1st quarter	Full moon	3rd quarter	New moon
Jan 6 ♈	Jan 13 ♋	Jan 21 ♏	Jan 29 ♒
Feb 5 ♉	Feb 12 ♌	Feb 20 ♐	Feb 28 ♓
Mar 6 ♊	Mar 14 ♍☍	Mar 22 ♑	Mar 29 ♈☌
Apr 5 ♋	Apr 13 ♎	Apr 21 ♒	Apr 27 ♉
May 4 ♌	May 12 ♏	May 20 ♒	May 27 ♊
June 3 ♍	June 11 ♐	June 18 ♓	June 25 ♋
July 2 ♎	July 10 ♑	July 18 ♈	July 24 ♌
Aug 1 ♏	Aug 9 ♒	Aug 16 ♉	Aug 23 ♍
Aug 31 ♐	Sep 7 ♓☍	Sep 14 ♊	Sep 21 ♍☌
Sep 29 ♑	Oct 7 ♈	Oct 13 ♋	Oct 21 ♎
Oct 29 ♒	Nov 5 ♉	Nov 12 ♌	Nov 20 ♏
Nov 28 ♓	Dec 4 ♊	Dec 11 ♍	Dec 20 ♐
Dec 27 ♈			

2025

2026

1st quarter	Full moon	3rd quarter	New moon
	Jan 3 ♋	Jan 10 ♎	Jan 18 ♑
Jan 26 ♉	Feb 1 ♌	Feb 9 ♏	Feb 17 ♒
Feb 24 ♊	Mar 3 ♍	Mar 11 ♐	Mar 19 ♓
Mar 25 ♋	Apr 2 ♎	Apr 10 ♑	Apr 17 ♈
Apr 24 ♌	May 1 ♏	May 9 ♒	May 16 ♉
May 23 ♍	May 31 ♐	June 8 ♓	June 15 ♊
June 21 ♎	June 29 ♑	July 7 ♈	July 14 ♋
July 21 ♎	July 29 ♒	Aug 6 ♉	Aug 12 ♌
Aug 20 ♏	Aug 28 ♓	Sep 4 ♊	Sep 11 ♍
Sep 18 ♐	Sep 26 ♈	Oct 3 ♋	Oct 10 ♎
Oct 18 ♑	Oct 26 ♉	Nov 4 ♌	Nov 9 ♏
Nov 17 ♒	Nov 24 ♊	Dec 1 ♍	Dec 9 ♐
Dec 17 ♓	Dec 24 ♋	Dec 30 ♎	

2027

1st quarter	Full moon	3rd quarter	New moon
			Jan 7 ♑
Jan 15 ♈	Jan 22 ♌	Jan 29 ♏	Feb 6 ♒
Feb 14 ♉	Feb 20 ♍	Feb 28 ♐	Mar 8 ♓
Mar 15 ♊	Mar 22 ♎	Mar 30 ♑	Apr 6 ♈
Apr 13 ♋	Apr 20 ♏	Apr 28 ♒	May 6 ♉
May 13 ♌	May 20 ♏	May 28 ♓	June 4 ♊
June 11 ♍	June 19 ♐	June 27 ♈	July 4 ♋
July 10 ♎	July 18 ♑	July 26 ♉	Aug 2 ♌
Aug 9 ♏	Aug 17 ♒	Aug 25 ♊	Aug 31 ♍
Sep 7 ♐	Sep 15 ♓	Sep 23 ♋	Sep 30 ♎
Oct 7 ♑	Oct 15 ♈	Oct 22 ♋	Oct 29 ♏
Nov 6 ♒	Nov 14 ♉	Nov 21 ♌	Nov 28 ♐
Dec 6 ♓	Dec 13 ♊	Dec 20 ♍	Dec 27 ♑

	1st quarter	Full moon	3rd quarter	New moon
	Jan 5 ♈	Jan 12 ♋♂°	Jan 18 ♎	Jan 26 ♒♂
	Feb 3 ♉	Feb 10 ♌	Feb 17 ♏	Feb 25 ♓
	Mar 4 ♊	Mar 11 ♍	Mar 17 ♐	Mar 26 ♈
	Apr 2 ♋	Apr 9 ♎	Apr 16 ♑	Apr 24 ♉
	May 2 ♌	May 8 ♏	May 16 ♒	May 24 ♊
2028	May 31 ♍	June 7 ♐	June 15 ♓	June 22 ♋
	June 29 ♎	July 6 ♑♂°	July 14 ♈	July 22 ♋♂
	July 28 ♏	Aug 5 ♒	Aug 13 ♉	Aug 20 ♌
	Aug 27 ♐	Sep 3 ♓	Sep 12 ♊	Sep 18 ♍
	Sep 25 ♑	Oct 3 ♈	Oct 11 ♋	Oct 18 ♎
	Oct 25 ♒	Nov 2 ♉	Nov 9 ♌	Nov 16 ♏
	Nov 24 ♓	Dec 2 ♊	Dec 9 ♍	Dec 16 ♐
	Dec 23 ♈	Dec 31 ♋♂°		

	1st quarter	Full moon	3rd quarter	New moon
			Jan 7 ♎	Jan 14 ♑♂
	Jan 22 ♉	Jan 30 ♌	Feb 5 ♏	Feb 13 ♒
	Feb 21 ♊	Feb 28 ♍⋅	Mar 7 ♐	Mar 15 ♓
	Mar 23 ♋	Mar 30 ♎	Apr 5 ♑	Apr 13 ♈
	Apr 21 ♌	Apr 28 ♏	May 5 ♒	May 13 ♉
2029	May 21 ♍	May 27 ♐	June 4 ♓	June 12 ♊♂
	June 19 ♍	June 26 ♑♂°	July 3 ♈	July 11 ♋♂
	July 18 ♎	July 25 ♒	Aug 2 ♉	Aug 10 ♌
	Aug 16 ♏	Aug 2 ♓	Sep 1 ♊	Sep 8 ♍
	Sep 15 ♐	Sep 22 ♓	Sep 30 ♋	Oct 7 ♎
	Oct 14 ♑	Oct 22 ♈	Oct 30 ♌	Nov 6 ♏
	Nov 13 ♒	Nov 21 ♉	Nov 28 ♍	Dec 5 ♐♂
	Dec 12 ♓	Dec 20 ♊♂°	Dec 28 ♎	

	1st quarter	Full moon	3rd quarter	New moon
				Jan 4 ♑
	Jan 11 ♈	Jan 19 ♋	Jan 26 ♏	Feb 2 ♒
	Feb 10 ♉	Feb 18 ♌	Feb 25 ♐	Mar 4 ♓
	Mar 12 ♊	Mar 19 ♍	Mar 26 ♑	Apr 2 ♈
	Apr 11 ♋	Apr 18 ♎	Apr 24 ♒	May 2 ♉
2030	May 10 ♌	May 17 ♏	May 24 ♓	June 1 ♊ σ
	June 9 ♍	June 15 ♐ ♂	June 22 ♈	June 30 ♋
	July 8 ♎	July 15 ♑	July 22 ♈	July 30 ♌
	Aug 6 ♏	Aug 13 ♒	Aug 21 ♉	Aug 28 ♍
	Sep 4 ♐	Sep 11 ♓	Sep 19 ♊	Sep 27 ♎
	Oct 4 ♑	Oct 11 ♈	Oct 19 ♋	Oct 26 ♏
	Nov 2 ♒	Nov 10 ♉	Nov 18 ♌	Nov 25 ♐ σ
	Dec 1 ♓	Dec 9 ♊ ♂	Dec 18 ♍	Dec 24 ♑
	Dec 31 ♈			

INDEX